AI
Transforming
Business

Corporate CxO Perspectives

Edited by
Georgios Kipouros
Daniel Pitchford

Published by Futurum Media Ltd, 2017
12 John Prince's Street
London W1G 0JR
AI Transforming Business ©Futurum Media Ltd, 2017
Project coordinated by Robert Woolliams
Cover design by Anil Karwal ©2017
Design and typesetting by Dolman Scott Ltd

.

ISBN: 978-1-5272-0868-1

Print
Dolman Scott Ltd
www.dolmanscott.com

Contents

Preface v

Introduction
Daniel Pitchford, Commercial Director, AI Business 1

Implementing AI, Beyond the Hype
Georgios Kipouros, Research & Content Director, AI Business............ 13

The Three 'A's of Artificial Intelligence
Josh Sutton, Global Head, Data and Artificial Intelligence,
Publicis.Sapient 25

Leading the Industrial Revolution with AI
Beena Ammanath, VP, Innovation, General Electric 33

*Is this the End of Work? How Machine Intelligence Will
Disrupt Jobs, Talent and Business Organization*
George Zarkadakis, Digital Lead, Willis Towers Watson 41

The Enterprise Path to AI
Kimberly Powell, Senior Director of AI and Deep Learning, NVIDIA ... 49

*When Artificial Intelligence is the Fastest Game in Town, Are
You In or Out?*
Jon Catling, Former Director, Global Data Architecture, Las Vegas Sands
Corporation 57

The Rebirth of the Financial Industry
Kumar Srivastava, VP, Products & Strategy, BNY Mellon 67

Creating Digital Assistants
Noel Lyons, Director of Digital Design, Barclays 79

Take Cover! How AI Will Upend Insurance, and Why that Matters for Us All
Simeon Preston, Group COO, AIA Group 95

Red Pill – Blue Pill
Marc Lien, Director of Innovation & Digital Development, Lloyds Banking Group 107

How Could Natural Language Dialogue Change the Future of Life and Business?
Michael Wei, Director of AI Research Center, Samsung 113

Cyber Security in the Age of Automation
Nicole Eagan, CEO, Darktrace 123

Autonomics and a Pro-Human Way
Kalyan Kumar, CTO, HCL Technologies 133

The Beginning of a New Era
Robert Woolliams, Head of Research, AI Business 145

Preface

London, May 2017

When AI Business launched back in 2014, Artificial Intelligence (AI) was not immediately associated with the business world. From machines taking human jobs, to robots taking over the world, a significant number of publications have since explored the potentially perilous advent of AI in the human realm.

In 2017, AI has become one of the hottest topics in the tech world, thanks to a more pragmatic approach that goes beyond Skynet scenarios. Business leaders are beginning to see tangible results from AI technologies; most if not all Fortune 1000 organizations have already embarked on an exciting journey that has the potential to create unprecedented efficiencies.

This is the first publication to focus on how corporate CxOs expect artificial intelligence to impact the business world. AI Business has partnered with 12 experts, all with senior positions in large and innovative organizations. The authors share a passion for the opportunity presented by AI, experience in implementing the still-nascent technology and a strong vision on how AI will shape the future of work. We are thankful to our authors for their time and contributions in sharing the positive side of AI.

AI Transforming Business aims to inspire the reader to get involved with AI by understanding its true potential for enhancing human productivity. The authors approach the topic from largely different angles; every chapter offers a plurality of views, examples, and expectations. A common denominator for all: the realization that there is significant substance behind the hype of AI.

Enjoy the read and join the world of intelligent opportunities!

Georgios Kipouros   Daniel Pitchford

Introduction

Daniel Pitchford, Commercial Director, AI Business

Daniel Pitchford serves as the Commercial Director of AI Business, the world's foremost online news publication focused specifically on how artificial intelligence is impacting the business landscape. His experience within the enterprise IT space spans many different technologies and market trends, and has positioned him at the center of a business community focused on future technology adoption. A degree in Mechanical Engineering combined with a commercial mindset is enabling Daniel – together with his AI Business team – to spot and exploit new trends within the technology space.

A brief history

Artificial Intelligence (AI) is far from a new phenomenon; indeed it has been around for many decades even before the pioneering work led by Alan Turing OBE back in the 1940s.

It was in fact centuries before that the idea of actually trying to build a machine to perform useful reasoning was first established, with Ramon Llull first developing the Calculus ratiocinator in 1300 CE. Later, Gottfried Leibniz built on Llull's concept and Whilhelm Shickard engineered the first calculating machine in 1623. Of course, these were very early and rudimentary examples of what later came in the 1900s.

Like Llull, Leibniz and Shickard, Turing was clearly a man ahead of his time, grappling with the question, 'could machines really think as a human?' – could they be programmed to emulate a human brain?

This led him to develop the now-famous 'Turing Test', which tests a machine's ability to exhibit intelligent behavior equivalent to, or indistinguishable from, that of a human.

It was indeed years later, in 1956 after Turing's unfortunate death, that the term 'Artificial Intelligence' was eventually coined by John McCarthy.

Investment poured into the research and development of AI throughout the 1960s, 70s, and 80s, backed by governments and corporates alike. However, despite the huge optimism of leading scientists, AI was not able to deliver on its promise. This led to what is now termed the 'AI Winter'. Funding for new projects slowed and both the US and British governments cut exploratory funding for AI research.

It wasn't until the late 90s where AI principles were being applied and used for more practical tasks including data mining and logistics that funding was fully restored. IBM famously developed Deep Blue, a machine that beat world chess champion Garry Kaspanov, and later Watson which would win the hit game show *Jeopardy!*[i]

How were these machines able to out-strategize and outthink the very best the human race had to offer in their respective fields?

The renaissance of AI

AI is certainly now the buzzword of technology, but why? As we've established, it is far from new – so what's different now? There are three fundamental pillars to why we're now experiencing a 'Big Bang' moment for AI.

The first is of course the more elaborate algorithms and mathematical approaches which have continued to be developed since the likes of Turing; as research continued to be deployed to the field, so too did more interest in developing more complex solutions.

The second is computational processing power; according to Moore's Law, processing capabilities have been doubling every two years, enabling faster data mining.

The third is the sheer amount of readily available data there is to actually process. Every day we create over 2.5 quintillion bytes of data, meaning more than 90% of the data in the world today has been created in the last two years alone. Mobile phones, social media, GPS, images, videos are among a few of the sources creating the vast amounts of data.

Defining AI in the 21st century

There are two main definitions of AI: 'General AI' and 'Narrow AI'.

The first relates to a machine's capability to perform any task that a human being can, which is what many people think of when hearing the term, thanks largely to Hollywood and science fiction.

Narrow AI, however, is a non-sentient artificial intelligence which is applied to a very specific or narrow task. This is where most interest has been paid in recent years and is why we're experiencing a renaissance in artificial intelligence in the corporate landscape.

AI is still an umbrella term for a range of underlying technologies, so there are a number of important terms which should be defined.

NLP, which stands for Natural Language Processing, enables computers to understand human language as it is spoken and written and to produce humanlike speech and writing. A machine is able to take unstructured data, process in a structured form, and then generate again in unstructured form which humans are able to understand. There are many companies focused on this technology across the spectrum of 'understanding', 'processing' and 'generation' of structured and unstructured data.

Machine Learning is a type of AI that involves using computerized mathematical algorithms that can learn from data and can depart from strictly following rules-based, pre-programmed logic. Machine learning algorithms typically build a probabilistic model and then use it to make assumptions and predictions about similar sets of data. The idea is for the machine to learn for itself, without the need for human intervention i.e. unsupervised machine learning. Currently, however, we're still very much seeing supervised machine learning in practice.

Deep Learning is a form of machine learning that uses the model of human neural nets to make predictions about new data sets in a hierarchical process. Many in the industry will argue that deep learning offers the more creative opportunities of the underlying technologies and is advancing other branches of AI. Leaders in deep learning include NVIDIA, who have pioneered GPU capabilities enabling even greater processing power.

Image Recognition refers to a machine's capability to identify images or objects, and process information based on an analysis of pattern identification. This is a powerful proposition for many large-scale enterprises, and there are many practical use cases in place already today; processing documents, for example, in the fraction of the time humans are able to do so and with much greater accuracy.

Automation, although not a specific AI technology itself, is the common goal of what enterprise AI technologies are geared toward. Automating tasks which humans would otherwise be completing, but in a far more efficient manner.

The realization of how AI will truly transform and power enterprises is now at the forefront of many business leader's minds. From the CEO, CIO, CTO, COO, CMO; boardrooms spanning the global Fortune 500 are hot with the discussion on how to leverage the opportunity AI presents for their organizations. Given the pervasive power of the technology, AI will certainly impact all business sectors.

Strategy is being set, partnerships forged, and markets established. Now is the time to join the AI revolution.

If we explore some of the earliest adopters of AI across key industry sectors, themes start to emerge that are being recognized by businesses globally.

Financial Services

Presenting arguably the biggest opportunity today for AI adoption and enterprise investment, financial services is an industry wide open to disruption from technology and through this has huge potential across a broad range of applications.

Investment in AI technologies within the finance sector is said to already be worth over $124m in 2017 (Tractica),[ii] and is increasing rapidly as more case studies emerge and appetite grows for leveraging the powerful solutions now coming to market.

Forecasts predict that investment will continue to grow over the short- and medium-term with investment levels to exceed $4.5bn by 2025 (Tractica).[iii]

There are a range of practical examples already taking shape today, across both consumer- and corporate-facing sides of financial institutions:

- Algorithmic trading
- Credit scoring/loan analysis
- Fraud prevention
- Risk assessment
- Customer experience
- Contact center automation
- Regulatory compliance

Banks are notably eager to utilise new AI products across a range of settings; Royal Bank of Scotland implemented Luvo, an AI chatbot to help with customer queries which would otherwise be left for customer care representatives to action alone. Luvo was initially rolled out online in December 2016 to help around 10% of the bank's SME customers. Other banks are also leveraging AI; Indian digibank has implemented KAI, an AI platform developed by Kasisto to handle customer queries that already manages over 95% of inbound calls. In partnership with IPsoft, the Swedish SEB introduced 'Amelia', an advanced virtual assistant bot which is set to help more than one million customers post-successful internal testing. Bank of America has also launched a chatbot named Erica. Themes are already emerging that reveal how ripe the appetite is among the industry's leading organizations.

Legal

Typically an industry slow to adopt to new technologies, the legal sector has conversely shown a readiness to adopt AI across some of the world's largest and prestigious firms. Magic Circle firm Allen & Overy has even set up a legal tech incubator to help innovate and adopt new technology across its practices.[iv] Berwin Leighton Paisner implemented an AI platform developed by RAVN Systems to create the UK's first 'contract robot'.[v] The platform converts unstructured data into structured output, in a fraction of the time required by a human and with a higher degree of accuracy.

Healthcare

Arguably the biggest opportunity for AI's transformative power to do good for the world is its use in the healthcare industry. It promises to enable huge medical advances, not only in accelerating the development of new medicines, but also in faster and more accurate diagnoses, meaning investment is ramping up from all sides of the eco-system.

Current investment in the sector sits at approximately $57m in 2017 but is set to climb to close to $3bn by 2025 (Tractica).[vi] The huge levels of investment in healthcare technology has been linked to the real need for reducing costs as well as the obvious benefits AI can offer in more accurate diagnoses and more personalized treatment plans.

Outside of process automation and administrative support, AI will also be valuable in medical research, investigating diseases, and creating new vaccines which will then be readily available.

Some of the practical use cases where AI is already being applied in the sector include:
- Drug discovery
- Clinical trials and compliance
- Medical diagnosis
- Personalized treatment plans
- Predicting patient outcomes
- Surgical processes
- Virtual assistants for doctors and contact centers

There are a number of pioneering technology companies specifically focused on applying AI in the healthcare sector.

Enlitic for example, is applying deep learning to large sets of medical images with the aim to find patterns in the data which would otherwise not be obvious to humans. Another business, AiCure, has created mobile apps which use image recognition to analyze patients' faces to identify if their medication is being taken correctly.

Arguably the leader in this space, IBM Watson has established an entire practice focused on the sector with Watson Health. Developing solutions which span life sciences, oncology, value-based care, and imaging, Watson Health has a growing number of partnerships with healthcare institutions globally. Partnerships with Pfizer and Barrow Neurological Institute to accelerate drug discovery and identifying new RNA-binding proteins linked to ALS are just a couple of the groundbreaking applications already in existence today.

Certainly, the broad range of applications within healthcare show great promise to revolutionize not only the sector but also our lives through the growing list of capabilities AI is advancing.

Retail

Another notable sector where AI is shaping an exciting future is retail. The sector's pioneers have been using primitive forms of AI for years for product recommendations and predictive analytics on churn and retention, however the future promises a far greater scale of opportunity.

Current investment is set to be worth over $50bn (Tractica) and predicted to rise exponentially with a CAGR of more than 55% over the next eight years.[vii]

The big questions being asked are around how to maximize the consumer's experience in unison with their spending capacity, and where AI fits into the proposition.

More powerful product recommendations through the use of conversational online assistants are one example. IBM Watson partnered with Fluid XPS to deliver an interactive shopping experience for customers of outdoor apparel retailer North Face.[viii] Thanks to NLP, shoppers are able to receive tailored recommendations in natural language as they shop, both enhancing their overall experience and also North Face's ability to influence customers' product choices.

Other applications include stock management, logistics, automated contact centers, personalized marketing and enhanced shopping experiences both online and in physical stores.

Horizontal

It is easy to see the vast range of use cases across all verticals, but it is also important to consider a more horizontal approach to how AI is being and can potentially be utilised.

Sales & marketing is a great example of how horizontal functions across all sectors can look to benefit from the new technology developments. Within marketing, AIM (Artificial

Intelligence Marketing) gives professionals a way to combine data science with campaign execution.[ix] Identifying key trends and valuable insights from data enables companies to better inform and in some cases automate future campaigns themselves.

Search, advertising, and customer service are three of the core components AIM is helping to improve. Analyzing customer search patterns is a great way for companies to better understand consumer behavior and thus to refine their campaigns.

More intelligent advertising has huge potential as consumers are becoming increasingly bombarded with adverts across many mediums; from TV, radio, social media, print, and mobile apps to name but a few. It is therefore vital to use the consumer's attention wisely; AIM makes this possible through more personalized adverts based on individual profiles. Campaigns launched at the most opportune time with the most personalized information are yielding both higher levels of spend and more frequent purchasing.

Beyond the core marketing applications, sales is another function where AI-enhanced tools are becoming common in the enterprise landscape. More intelligent CRM platforms from industry heavyweights including Salesforce and Oracle are helping sales professionals to automate administrative tasks and also develop more intelligent sales campaigns for targeting prospects.

Horizontal applications will therefore continue to evolve through a wide spectrum of business functions, both through internal and external capacities.

i   https://aibusiness.com/ibm-watson-exclusive-interview-with-european-director-paul-chong/

ii   https://www.tractica.com/research/artificial-intelligence-for-enterprise-applications/

iii   https://www.tractica.com/research/artificial-intelligence-for-enterprise-applications/

iv   http://www.globallegalpost.com/big-stories/allen--overy-launches-legaltech-incubator-93101223/

v   https://www.ravn.co.uk/ravn-systems-artificial-intelligence-platform-deployed-successfully-berwin-leighton-paisner/

vi   https://www.tractica.com/research/artificial-intelligence-for-enterprise-applications/

vii   https://www.tractica.com/research/artificial-intelligence-for-enterprise-applications/

viii   https://www.forbes.com/sites/kimberlywhitler/2016/12/01/how-artificial-intelligence-is-changing-the-retail-experience-for-consumers/#637ff0051008

ix   https://www.emarsys.com/en-uk/resources/blog/artificial-intelligence-marketing-in-2017/

Implementing AI, Beyond the Hype

**Georgios Kipouros, Research & Content Director,
AI Business**

---

*Georgios Kipouros is the Research & Content Director of AI
Business. Georgios has over 11 years' experience in the media
& conference sector, specializing in enterprise technology. He
was previously Managing Director at Osney Media Ltd, Head of
Production for the Cloud World Series at Informa, and Research
Manager for IIR Telecoms & Technology events. Georgios has
also worked for the European Commission and JEF in Brussels
with experience in digital innovation and regulation. He holds a
First Class Msc in Development Economics & Communication
from LSE and a mini-MBA from London Business School.*

Artificial intelligence is poised to be the biggest technological
hype of 2017. Conversations around the renaissance of AI
technologies and their impact in the world of work have
dominated events and a wide range of both niche and
mainstream publications. The dominant angle has been the
impact on employment, with automation of jobs a pivotal
theme.

There is an acute need for a pragmatic, facts-based approach
to how AI is tangibly transforming business today and how
it will evolve in the future. Between January and March
2017, AI Business set out to research Fortune 500 global

businesses, surveying C-Suite executives about how they see AI impacting their organizations, understanding their current and future AI projects, concerns and overall strategy. The comprehensive survey deciphers the perspectives of hundreds of senior corporate executives on how AI is transforming their organizations.

Is this a big deal?

There is real substance behind the hype: AI is becoming central to the corporate agenda, as survey results clearly demonstrate.

Over 95% of corporate leaders surveyed recognize AI as a pivotal issue: they agree it will transform their industry; 98% perceive it as essential for their organization. More than 80% compare the impact of AI to that of the internet, with less than 10% still believing that the impact of AI is more hype than essence.

Machine learning and deep learning dominates current investment in AI with over 80% of Europe's leading organizations investing in the technology. Natural language processing (NLP) is also popular with 56% engaged in this sector. An average of €4million per AI project is expected to be spent within the next two years, soaring to over €30million in a five-year term.

Where is the impact?

What does AI practically mean to their organization? 'Increased productivity, process efficiencies and optimization of activity are the three key areas of impact,' highlights Periklies Antoniou of Diageo. Moreover, 92% of respondents see AI bringing improved efficiency across the board, 77% expect to see a reduction in overall costs while 66% also anticipate enhanced accuracy in their operations. Interestingly, 28% believe that AI will enable humans to make the most of their creative side by removing mundane tasks that will be done more efficiently without human intervention.

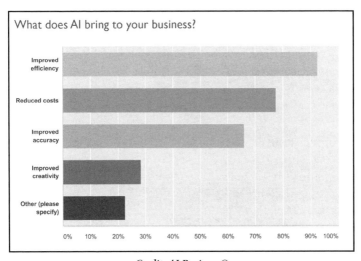

Credit: AI Business©

In terms of individual business functions, over 85% of respondents see data collection & management as the domain that AI will revolutionize. It is indeed in this area that most organizations have already started investing, with machine learning and deep learning projects making the most of organizations' Big Data. Further still, business leaders expect a significant impact of AI in customer

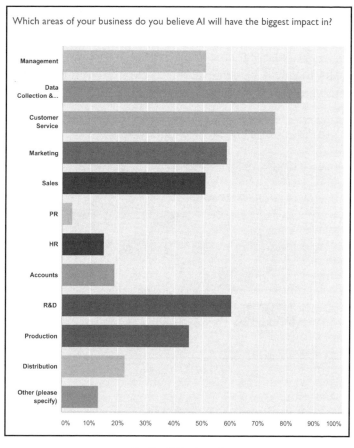

Credit: AI Business©

service – a function that applies to all organizations and one that is particularly difficult to 'get right'. From NLP to image recognition, organizations are using a wide range of AI tools to improve and strengthen their relationship with the customer. R&D and marketing are very close as the third and fourth areas singled out by approximately 60% of respondents, followed by sales and management, which was identified by about 50% of respondents as functions that will drastically change through the advent of AI. This publication includes numerous practical examples of how all the aforementioned areas will be impacted by AI.

Change is also happening across the organization's structure as a result of AI. Over 80% of respondents expect a major change to business structures, roles and hierarchies with the development and increased implementation of AI technologies. As has been widely reported, a number of jobs will eventually be automated. George Zarkadakis of Willis Towers Watson is, nonetheless, confident that a significant number of new roles will be created as a result of AI being implemented; according to IBM Watson's Rob Morris we will witness a shift rather than a net loss of jobs as a result of AI.

Who is responsible for AI within an organization?

Internal transformation is also happening across organizations. 'Artificial intelligence will change everything' asserts Neil Pearce, Group CIO at Travis Perkins. A plethora of new roles and hierarchies are appearing – from board-level Chief AI officers to enhanced Chief Data Officers.

Georgios Kipouros

Asking respondents to identify those driving AI projects produced nebulous results. While initially considered an area of interest to the CTO/Head of IT, just 19% of respondents recognize them as currently responsible for AI - a tie with the CIO function. Chief Digital/Data officers also take a lead in just over one in ten organizations, a similar figure to that of the CEO. Interestingly, over 30% of respondents identify different roles leading AI projects; from Heads of Transformation to Directors of R&D, over 32 job titles were shared by our respondents as executives driving AI adoption in their organization.

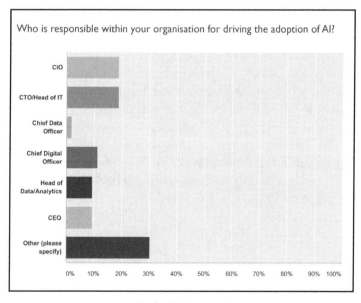

Credit: AI Business©

An important addition in this conversation is the question of talent. Over 79% of senior executives highlighted the lack of available talent as one of the main obstacles in implementing AI – data scientists and machine learning experts are in short supply and highly sought-after. A broader, all-encompassing conversation on talent in the era of AI is pivotal; organizations will be forced to address the skills gap sooner rather than later.

What are the challenges?

There are a number of further bumps in the road to adopting AI. The amorphous regulatory framework is one that concerns over half of respondents – who regulates, and what kind of rules should we expect? The ethical challenges and risks of using AI are also on the CxO's agenda. Surprisingly, the single biggest obstacle to AI adoption highlighted by 67% of respondents is the lack of understanding about AI's capabilities or limitations; despite the hype, knowledge on the opportunity around AI is still rather limited.

The lack of understanding is coupled with a significant lack of talent able to drive AI projects. As mentioned above, AI experts are at a significant premium with strong competition among large corporates for the finest minds in the field.

Security of information and data handled through AI is a significant concern raised by over 60% of respondents. Liability when machines make mistakes and the potential to lose control over AI's capabilities are ethical issues that have also been brought forward by over half of senior executives surveyed.

Perhaps to the surprise of mainstream media outlets, only 35% of respondents see AI's impact on employment as a stumbling block; the view that a number of new roles will be created as others are automated is one shared by many CxO leaders and most of our book's contributors.

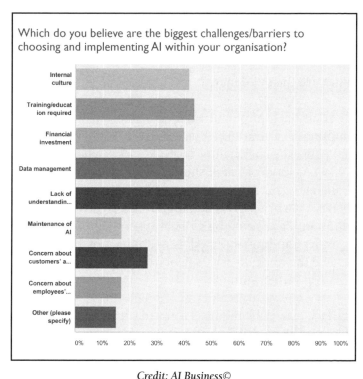

Credit: AI Business©

Who is the preferred AI vendor partner?

Although AI is often classed as an 'emerging' technology, the solution providers deemed to be leading innovation in the space come as no surprise. When asked to identify the top vendors in artificial intelligence, respondents rank Google, Amazon, IBM Watson, Microsoft and Facebook as the top five, in that order. All five have made bold, public announcements in support of AI's potential for transforming the business world. Google's CEO predicts a shift from a mobile-first to an AI-first world within the next decade;[i] Microsoft's Satya Nadella sees the need for AI to be adopted for helping as many people as possible;[ii] IBM's Ginny Rometty confirms that AI is here to stay.[iii] Many

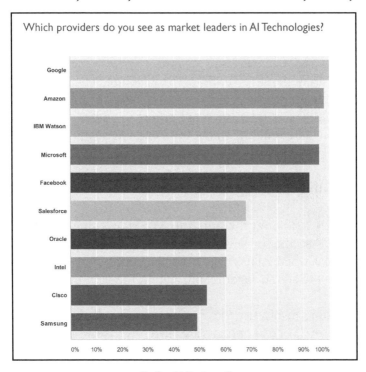

Credit: AI Business©

more leading technology vendors like Oracle, Cisco, SAP will be joining the AI conversation with bold products and services expected this year. The world's leading technology vendors maintain the long-term view that

AI will dominate discussions with their enterprise clients for years to come.

Complementing the tech giants, a rich ecosystem of AI start-ups has emerged, spanning the Silicon Valley to Shenzen to Shoreditch. A vivid M&A landscape is sustained by the groundbreaking pace of innovation in this space – from DeepMind (Google) to Saffron (Intel) and Implisit (Salesforce), tech giants are racing to acquire the next AI pioneer.

'We think that the technology isn't completely mature yet but that we have to get on the AI train now,' Marion Aubert, working on IT Innovation at Burberry, concludes. Indeed, vendors are building the AI train and its wagons while the enterprise drivers are gearing up for their next journey.

Investing for the AI future

Is ROI visible on the horizon? While less than 30% are already seeing some ROI on their investments – particularly in areas where AI has been used in CEM & CRM – over half expect to see stronger results within the next three years.

The sums involved in these investments are also noteworthy; while 40% of respondents are currently investing less than €500,000 in each AI project, this figure is expected to soar to over €3million per project in the next three to five years.

Michael Natusch, newly appointed as Global Head of AI for Prudential, believes AI will have a revolutionary impact in his organization. AI Business' own research confirms that the hype is based on solid foundations, promising investments and genuine business value. Enterprise CxOs do recognize the opportunity in place. AI is still a work in progress, but the fourth industrial revolution is happening now and transforming the future of business.

i   https://www.entrepreneur.com/article/274922
ii   https://news.microsoft.com/europe/2017/01/17/democratizing-ai-satya-nadella-shares-vision-at-dld/
iii http://uk.businessinsider.com/ginni-rometty-on-ibm-watson-and-ai-2015-5

The Three 'A's of Artificial Intelligence

Josh Sutton, Global Head, Data and Artificial Intelligence, Publicis.Sapient

Josh Sutton is the Global Head of Publicis.Sapient's Data and Artificial Intelligence Practice. In this role, he is responsible for leveraging Big Data tools as well as correlation-based and causal-based AI platforms to help clients transform their businesses. He works closely with clients to ensure that Publicis.Sapient align the right tools and platforms with clients' business objectives.

Josh also serves as a member of the executive leadership team for Publicis.Sapient's Business Transformation Services group. This group is focused on helping clients identify and capitalize on opportunities to transform their business. Josh joined Sapient in 1995. Josh serves on the board of directors for NPower, a New York-based non-profit focused on mobilizing the tech community and providing individuals, non-profits and schools the access and opportunity to build tech skills and achieve their potential.

Artificial intelligence (AI) is the most powerful enabler of transformation since the internet. Not only is it rapidly changing the way that businesses operate, but it is also expected to have a material impact on the way that societies function and countries engage with one another. Artificial intelligence has been one of the most talked about topics at the World Economic Forum's conference in Davos for both 2016 and 2017. The question that many people are asking, however, is exactly how artificial intelligence will impact their lives. To answer that question, we first need to understand what is actually transforming in society today.

A current world of transformation

We are living in the midst of one of the most rapid transformations that the world has ever seen. This has been powered by a number of technologies – first the internet, then mobility, and most recently artificial intelligence. When you take away the individual technology enablers, however, the transformation is much more basic in nature. As a global society, we are in the process of evolving from a product-based marketplace to a service-based marketplace. The companies that are succeeding in the global economy are not those with the best product, but rather those that excel at fulfilling a customer's desired experience, regardless of whether that customer is a single person or a large enterprise.

The implications of this are profound:

1. The market capitalization per employee is significantly higher than it has ever been before. In 2006, the two companies with the highest market capitalizations in the world (Exxon Mobil and GE) employed approximately 400,000 people. In 2016, a decade later, the two companies with the highest market capitalization (Apple and Google) employed approximately 180,000 people – less than half of their counterparts from the prior decade. It should also be noted that the combined value

of Apple and Google in 2016 was roughly 1.5 times that of Exxon Mobil and GE in 2006.

2. There is a dramatic increase in the volatility of market leaders. On average, a company is being removed from the S&P 500 every two weeks. This is a rate of disruption that is faster than any time in history. While the average lifespan of an S&P 500 company was once 75 years, it has been reduced to a mere 15 years today and appears on track to continue to shrink.

3. The companies that are disrupting the markets today are not relying on any production capabilities, but rather are focused on providing the best possible service. Examples of this include Uber, Airbnb, and Amazon.

Artificial intelligence will accelerate transformation

It is reasonable to believe that as we look to the future, this transformation to a service-based economy will continue to accelerate. Given this thesis, the question is: "How will AI serve to enable and empower this shift?" To answer this question, we first need to acknowledge that there is no single type of technology or business process that is implied when people talk about 'artificial intelligence'. Instead, there are a multitude of different types of technology which all serve to replicate or enhance activities that we traditionally associate with human beings. These range from analyzing data to engaging in a conversation to performing tasks based on a set of common-sense rules. This leads us to the three 'As of AI: Amplification, Articulation, and Automation.

Amplification

Machine learning, inclusive of all of its various subdomains such as deep learning, is providing us with the ability to dramatically amplify our ability to extract insights from data and perform complex tasks at scale. This amplification of our intelligence is enabling individuals to perform tasks that normally would require teams of people. In some cases, work is being performed that had previously been impossible simply because of the scale and complexity of the data. One relevant example of this is in marketing. Historically, people have been viewed as segments and analyzed as large groups. This was done simply because humans don't have the time or cognitive capability to review the actions of every individual person and determine the best way to reach that specific person. That has changed with the advent of machine learning. Advertising will never be the same, since brands can now leverage AI to understand the specific actions that are driving an individual's behavior and craft bespoke messages for them at the right time to influence their actions. This augmentation of man-plus-machine is creating better results across a wide range of industries, including finance, healthcare, energy, and retail.

Articulation

Natural language understanding technologies (NLU) are changing the way that we engage with technology. While we have historically had to deal with clumsy interfaces that attempt to convert our intentions into a set of discrete binary decisions and data elements, the advent of NLU technologies are enabling us to talk to technology in the same way that we talk to one another. This shift in engagement is already starting to redefine customer channels, with over 2000 chatbots having been launched in the past year. Moving forward, the role of digital assistants powered by NLU technologies promises to redefine how we engage with brands through always-on platforms that are ready to listen to our needs and respond accordingly.

Automation

The automation of knowledge work, ranging from basic approaches such as robotic process automation (RPA) through to advanced combinations of multiple types of technology, are changing the economics associated with nearly every business model. Just as robotics changed the economics of manufacturing, the automation of knowledge work will transform traditional knowledge-based industries such as the law, medicine and finance. While in most cases entire jobs will not be fully automated, specific tasks within the scope of a job today will be automated. This will lead to a dramatic increase in efficiency and a change in the economics associated with most industries. In addition, there will be some jobs which might cease to exist in the form that we know them today – the most widely cited example of this is that of truck and car drivers, who are likely to be replaced by autonomous vehicles. While there will likely be societal impacts that are felt in many different ways over the coming years, there is little doubt that a large portion of the work that is performed by humans today will be automated in the coming years.

The AI-enabled global society of the future

Each of these three 'A's is remarkably powerful in its own right, but the global society of the future will be led by the companies and countries which combine these to maximize their ability to serve both customers and citizens.

The technology industry is evolving rapidly and there does not appear to be a single provider of choice when it comes to AI technologies. Even more importantly, the data that many firms will rely on is held in a variety of different locations. The natural conclusion that can be drawn from this is that, in order to build a compelling service for the future, you must approach your design with a component-based mentality. The ability to switch-out technology and data providers as the world evolves will be critical to your ongoing success. It is not possible to overstate the importance of developing a comprehensive technology infrastructure that enables access to a wide variety of changing data sources, machine learning engines, natural language understanding tools, and process automation technologies.

Tomorrow's market leaders will be those that can best leverage these technologies to provide innovative and compelling services that make society better than it is today. Artificial intelligence is the cornerstone of the fourth industrial revolution. Just as with every preceding industrial revolution, we can expect that there will be dramatic changes in the types of jobs that we perform and how we work together as a global society. We can also expect that the leaders of the coming decades will be those that capitalize on the potential of these technological advances to provide materially improved services – not those that simply seek to do the same thing that they do today at a lower price point or faster timescale. As a caterpillar transforms into a butterfly with an entirely new and improved means of travelling, so will tomorrow's leaders provide new and improved services to humankind.

Leading the Industrial Revolution with AI

Beena Ammanath, VP, Innovation, General Electric

Beena Ammanath is a thought-leader in the field of the application of artificial intelligence for the industrial domain. She is an award-winning technology executive leader whose work has shaped the usage of data, analytics and AI at several corporations. Beena won the 2016 CIO-Drexel Analytics 50 award for being one of the top 50 global innovators in data science, was named as one of the 2017 top eight female analytics experts by Forbes and named by the San Francisco Business Times as one of the 2017 Most Influential Women in Bay Area.

Beena is the founder and CEO of The Women in AI movement. She has also worked at several recognized international organizations: British Telecom, E*trade, Thomson Reuters, Bank of America and also, Silicon Valley start-ups, in engineering and management positions. She is currently the Vice President of Innovation at General Electric. Beena is also a Board Director at ChickTech, an organization focused on increasing and retaining diversity in tech.

The origins of artificial intelligence (AI) as a concept can be traced as far back as the ancient Greek mythologies. Though AI as a science was not coined until 1956 at the Dartmouth Conference, the idea of AI has always been in the imagination of humans. And AI has several definitions too. In my view,

AI can be defined as a machine smarter than the best human brains in every aspect and every field, including scientific, artistic, general knowledge and social skills.

Over the past century, we have been through several hype cycles of AI with over-promise, over-investment, under-delivery, and investment reduction. Today, the technology advancements in Big Data technologies, cheap massively scalable infrastructure, and storage is helping us tremendously to tackle bigger and bolder problems in AI than ever before. Every company, every domain is looking at leveraging AI to improve its business value.

Industrial systems provide the perfect domain for experimenting with AI techniques. Since it's a controlled environment to a large extent, many of the tasks are well-defined and have been in action for a longer period of time; the risk can be controlled and measured as well. The challenges of optimizing and scheduling factory operations are well-defined.

AI in the factory

When we think about AI in a factory today, we visualize robots – that's our image of AI in a factory. But it is so much more than that. Over the past few decades, industrial robots have replaced humans in most of the repetitive jobs in factories. We have come a long way since the first industrial revolution.

The first industrial revolution involved the transition to new manufacturing processes – this included going from hand-production methods to machines, the increased use of steam power, and the rise of the factory system. The second industrial revolution leveraged the advancements in railroad networks and telegraph lines to globalize manufacturing, leading to unprecedented movement of people and ideas, assembly-line manufacturing and mass production. The third industrial revolution was really about digitization. In the mid-60s, the first batch of industrial robots made their appearance to replace the human workers who did the repetitive task of assembling a product part as it rolled down the assembly line. But the early robots were primarily dumb machines that could perform a single task only. AI is going to change that in a big way.

Any factory system has the following key pillars: design, manufacturing, supply chain, distribution and services. As software and AI become more mainstream, each one of those key areas will have a huge impact over the next decade.

Design

In the past, designs on paper were not only cumbersome and tedious to maintain, but collaboration across different design teams was nearly impossible. So you would see different engineering teams within the same company spending an equal amount of time and brainpower to create a similar design.

Today, thanks to digitization, a large part of design has moved from designs on paper to designs using software and digital tools. This makes it easy to collaborate across departments, across geographies and across cross-functional teams. Additive manufacturing is a whole new way of rapid prototyping, leading to faster iterations around fine-tuning the design of a part or an assembly of parts.

Design is where AI will be pushed to its limits. Even though we have digitized the processes behind design, it still takes a human to design the next cool part or an entire product. AI would have reached its true potential when a machine can design the next killer product, all its components and parts. Just as a human receives feedback about the current product from the field or from the manufacturing plant or the reliability tests and redesigns the product with a better material or a better alignment between the individual parts of the product – can an AI-enabled machine do the same? Can AI design the next new product in a product line?

Manufacturing

Manufacturing factories have become so much more efficient today, and it's largely due to digitization – and robots. Today, robots are taking over a lot of the tasks on the factory floor that are repetitive and do not require any human brainpower. In Europe, we have just started to see AI run factories for weeks without any human supervisors – a truly autonomous manufacturing plant. We are also seeing production equipment becoming smarter and more flexible. Whether it is robots equipped with sensing systems that enable automated milling machines to swap their own tools and cuts in multiple directions; or production processes enabling the standardization of parameters of certain components to drive the standardization of production lines at all factories; AI will soon allow any factory to produce locally what its local market needs.

AI will empower small and midsize companies to launch new and innovative products faster and in a cheaper manner. Today, we are already beginning to see the disruptive emergence of what is being termed as 'social manufacturing': communities offering 3D printing and other manufacturing services very similar to the social media impact.

Manufacturing was one of the first use cases for AI deployment and is allowing goods to be manufactured more economically, in smaller numbers and with less labor. Manufacturing is almost coming full circle, moving away from mass production and towards much more customized production.

Supply chain

Supply chain can be an all-encompassing function within an industrial manufacturing organization. For the purpose of this chapter, let's define supply chain as all the activities involving sourcing, procurement of materials needed for manufacturing, logistics and collaboration with channel partners. Essentially, it's integrating the supply and demand management within and across companies.

Today, industrial companies are busy digitizing their supply chains to differentiate and drive revenue growth. We have put in solutions to compare current business conditions with historical ones and forecast what's likely to happen next and act accordingly. We are moving from insights into supplies to leveraging insights from demand.

Artificial intelligence will be crucial in shaping the future of supply chain. With the continued progress in the development and use of driverless autonomous vehicles, logistics will undergo a fundamental change. Artificial intelligence will be handling most, if not all, of the domestic and international movement of goods. Think of AI-managed warehouses with autonomous forklifts. And AI-driven cost-reduction techniques driving the best pricing across multiple suppliers. And real-time AI technologies that analyze procurement requests, tender and workflow approvals tied with the sourcing employees' external data along with HR and financial data to identify and prevent any compliance issues in a few seconds. The day is not far off when AI will take over most of the demand planning and procurement activities.

Services

After a machine (a manufactured item like a jet engine or a locomotive or a tractor) is delivered to the end customer, a large effort goes into servicing and maintaining those machines. It could be planned servicing or unplanned servicing. Planned servicing is mostly built into the contracts or sales agreements and is more cost-effective overall for the industrial company, as it can be optimized from a time and resource perspective. Unplanned servicing has a negative impact overall, from both the customer and manufacturer's perspectives. It can result in downtime and delays for the end customer.

For both planned and unplanned servicing, it can be done in the field – where the machine is actually located – or it can be brought into the factory for servicing. A number of factors drive that decision.

Today, a large effort is being put in by all manufacturers to reduce unplanned servicing. With the power of data and analytics, today we are able to predict when a machine or one of its parts might fail and proactively fix the issue. Today, a machine-learning algorithm can predict the failure likelihood of, say, a part within a wind turbine in a remote location, and a field service engineer is sent out to the turbine with the new part or has the know-how to repair the part once he or she is there.

Very soon, we will see AI taking servicing to a whole new level. The human field service engineer will not have to physically travel to the remote sites. To start with, there will be smart drones that can travel to the location and replace the part – these will be programmed to have the know-how to repair the parts too.

But AI will have its true impact when the machine itself becomes self-healing. Think of a self-maintaining power grid system that needs no human interventions. Or a self-diagnosing, self-healing jet engine that repairs itself mid-air for minor repairs and goes into the servicing center/factory/ shop only for major repairs. Just as a human would be able to Band-Aid a minor cut, but goes in to meet the surgeon when deeper expertise is needed.

Evolution of AI

The big question that all this raises is: when will computers be able to emulate humans, become self-aware, intelligent and creative?

There is a lot of hype today that we are on the verge of building a machine that can do everything a human brain can. However, if you dig deeper into that claim, you learn that it is still hype. We are a long way away from developing a machine brain with human intelligence and capabilities. Very little and slow progress is being made on this front. To design something that equals or surpasses the human brainpower is just not physically possible with today's technology.

For now, humans and machines will have to work in partnership to drive the best outcomes. Machines will be able to provide a level of expertise that can help humans perform more efficiently and effectively.

From an industrial manufacturing company perspective, AI will link design engineering, manufacturing, supply chain, distribution and services intelligently. There will still be robots, but the robots will do much more than what they do today. There will still be humans, but they will do much more than what they do today. The machines and humans together will self-improve products and processes within an industrial system to drive the fourth industrial revolution.

Is this the End of Work? How Machine Intelligence Will Disrupt Jobs, Talent and Business Organization

George Zarkadakis, Digital Lead, Willis Towers Watson

George Zarkadakis is the Director of Willis Towers Watson's Digital Incubator; as well as the leader of the Future of Work Strategy Advisory Services for GB and Western Europe. He has over 25 years' experience in management consulting, media, marketing and communications, as well as in digital strategy and innovation. He holds a PhD in artificial intelligence and is the author of "In Our Own Image: will Artificial Intelligence Save Us or Destroy Us?" (Rider Books). He blogs regularly in the Huffington Post on artificial intelligence and the fourth industrial revolution.

We are witnessing the beginning of a new industrial revolution where the nature of machines changes in a profound way: they increasingly acquire characteristics and behaviors that we usually associate with human intelligence. The key driving technology is machine learning (ML), or algorithms that enable computers to infer facts out of data, and thus improve their performance over time. What makes this technology pivotal to economic transformation is its uncanny timing. Businesses, governments, scientific organizations, and each and every one of us individually are nowadays swimming – or perhaps 'drowning' – in oceans of data. Research from IDC suggests that data will grow 100-fold, from 4.4ZB today to 44ZB by 2020.[i] While business processes were at the heart of the first wave of computer automation in the 1970s and 80s, now it is mostly about the data. Machine learning is key to dealing with the data deluge, and – more importantly – to drawing value from this newly-found bounty.

The robots are coming!

Nevertheless, the universal impetus to make machines capable of understanding has an obvious repercussion: what would be the role of humans in a world run by intelligent machines? This is not a novel question. It was first posed during the first industrial revolution when machines began to transform the cotton industry in Great Britain. Interestingly, the cause of social reaction then was not that automation replaced humans, but because it replaced skilled labor with unskilled labor. Indeed, that was the economic drive for investing in the new machines; namely, lower cost of wages and a bigger pool of labor to select from. Automation tends to 'hollow out' mid-skilled jobs while leaving low- and high-skilled jobs relatively unaffected. Could history repeat itself in the 21st century? Or are highly-skilled jobs now also prone to cognitive automation?

Certain economic research points very much towards that. In their 2013 paper, 'The Future of Employment', economists C. Frey and M. Osborne argued that 47%

of current jobs in the US will be fully automated in the next 10 years.[ii] But more nuanced research that followed took a different approach. Instead of examining whole occupations, jobs were deconstructed into tasks and a probability for automation was assigned at tasks. Thus, a team of researchers from McKinsey surmized that only 5% of jobs will be fully automated[iii], while an OECD team argued that on average 9% of jobs will be fully automated.[iv] Nevertheless, all research points to the fact that most of the jobs will be disrupted to a varying degree because of cognitive automation. The degree of disruption will depend upon many factors, and vary according to industry. For example, manufacturing has been automating for decades now. The sharp fall of robot cost is causing the onshoring of many manufacturing processes; however, that does not mean the creation of new manufacturing jobs. A fully automated factory is the direction of the current journey. Similarly, logistics and transportation seem to be among the industries where robots will increasingly play a role. Amazon is already using the Kivo robots to reengineer its order fulfilment processes,[v] while Otto (a company acquired by Uber) has demonstrated the first fully autonomous truck.[vi]

But how about other industries? In order to understand the future of work in the age of intelligent machines, it is important to place change in context, and view in relation to other 'moving parts' in the economy.

Forces of change: AI and the gig economy

In a world of income inequality, the problem of low human productivity is often mentioned as the root of all political evil.

It is true that low productivity is at the heart of persistently stagnant wages. But it is also the reason why new jobs are being constantly created. Artificial intelligence could potentially augment human productivity, which will have both a positive as well as a negative impact on the job market. Of course, this is an argument that we have heard before: computers were supposed to increase human productivity, only they didn't. As Nobel Laureate Robert Solow famously quipped in 1987, "you can see the computer age everywhere but in the productivity statistics".[vii] The 2015 Economic Report of the President calculated that if productivity growth had continued at its 1948-1973 pace for the past 40 years, the average household's income would be $30,000 higher today.[viii] This time, however, promises to be different, if only because ML allows the production of new value from an untapped resource: data. What is also new and different from before is that 'jobs' are not what they used to be, i.e. stable things that underscored a life-time contract between employer and employee. According to data from the US Department of Labor, around 40% of the US workforce is currently working in the gig economy[ix], and the trend is increasing. Further to that, our relationship with work is no longer binary: free agents or contractors may be working for a single company just like full-time employees. Think, for example, of workers in platforms such as Uber or Deliveroo. It is very likely that the current regulatory vacuum will soon be filled in order to account for these new forms of work, and to provide solutions to the many challenges around pensions, insurance, leave, and health coverage. Governments are motivated to bridge the current regulatory gap because of lost tax revenues, as well as increased liabilities in public finances that must fund pensions and healthcare.

Given the trend towards more democratized forms of employment, ML provides new opportunities, and challenges, to organizations as well as workers. Companies will need to rethink how they attract, manage and retain talent; but also how to leverage the benefits and costs of talent on-demand and task automation. There are obvious benefits to work automation; for example, reduction of cost and increased speed to capability. Automating repetitive, routine cognitive tasks frees experienced worker time and allows them to be more creative and productive. Opting for talent on-demand reduces the cost of recruiting and onboarding and increases speed of capability, particularly in time-critical projects such as digital transformation. Talent platforms also solve the problem of skills obsolescence, particularly with technology skills. But there are significant risks involved as well. How can companies decide what skillset they should keep and what to outsource? And how about work automation: where is benefit maximized, and what are the criteria for strategizing on talent? For some jobs artificial intelligence will be transformative, i.e. it will change the job in a radical way, eliminate the need for it, or possibly reinvent it. But for most jobs the effect of AI will be 'augmentative', by enabling higher productivity and creativity. But how can leaders distinguish between the two scenarios?

Transformative vs augmentative disruption

As AI and ML applications become pervasive, questions arise with regards to rationalizing jobs and managing human talent. Businesses must decide how to maximize the benefit of automating work tasks using intelligent machines, while at the same time manage the risk of automating too fast or too slow.

A useful criterion for analyzing the impact of automation on jobs is to distinguish categories of possible outcomes. The first category would be jobs that are *transformed* by machine intelligence. Take for example the job of a maintenance engineer who performs physical inspections of installations, or equipment, on a periodic or emergency basis. As things become intelligent and interconnected via the Internet of Things (IoT) this job will be profoundly transformed. There will be little or no need for physical inspection. Instead there will be streams of data coming from equipment and installations that need to be analyzed. Therefore, the maintenance engineer will need a new set of skills, such as data analytics, in order to perform the transformed role. Perhaps he would also need to learn how to program a robot, or a drone, which will perform a physical inspection whenever the data predicts a possible failure.

The other category of jobs will be ones that are *augmented* by machine intelligence. A typical example for this category would be any customer-facing job. Imagine a restaurant where the waiters have access to customer data in real time, via perhaps a Google Glass-like interface. Machine intelligence will be used to analyze customer data and suggest a personalized experience, which then the "augmented waiter" can deliver. No need to puzzle over a menu, or feeling apprehensive about which wine to choose, your augmented waiter will be able to suggest exactly what would make you happier, as if he/she had known you forever!

Finally, there will be completely *new jobs* that will need to be created in the new economy of the fourth industrial revolution. It is probably impossible to guess what those jobs might be. Who could have foreseen the need for mobile application engineers ten years ago? Perhaps ten years from now we will need "robot ethicists" to ensure that intelligent machines behave in a way that aligns with our values. Or, perhaps, we will need professionals who combine psychology with coding skills to furnish robots and digital assistants with human-like personalities.

Future-proofing your business

Cognitive automation is ushering in a new industrial revolution. Predicting the outcome of this social, economic and industrial disruption is impossible. Nevertheless, companies can begin to adapt and prepare for this future by recognizing the forces of change and developing the appropriate strategies. To begin, companies should analyze their current job structures and begin to think around tasks and skills. Work assignment needs to transform and become dispersed and project-bound. A great model for such a transformation already exists and is called 'agile methodology'. What is exciting about agile is the potential to scale this way of product delivery across the whole of an organization. The challenges for doing so are many; so many companies are evaluating scaling agile by piloting a more agile business process.

Organizational change is a continuous process, and one that is likely to accelerate as the fourth industrial revolution begins to disrupt traditional business models. Matrix organizations are not very flexible when it comes to making the most of agile ways of working. A more networked approach is required in order to create a highly responsive organization that innovates and competes.

Finally, rewarding work will have to undergo a radical reinvention. The gig economy is challenging the binary employee-contractor paradigm. In this new world of new working relationships, personalization is the key to achieving loyalty and fairness. Data and ML will define talent analytics, and HR professionals will have to acquire many of the skills that marketers now have. Business leaders may need to rethink their organizations like platforms, rather than self-contained and impermeable organizational entities. In this futuristic scenario, a company's value is contingent on how effectively it can harness human talent, not necessarily hire it. Artificial intelligence will be key to the success of such future organizations because of the importance of data as well as of cognitive automation. So it makes sense that AI becomes part of core company strategy today, and that the right skills are found that can lead the organizational change that will be required.

---

[i] http://www.computerweekly.com/news/2240217788/Data-set-to-grow-10-fold-by-2020-as-internet-of-things-takes-off

[ii] "The Future of Employment", by C. Frey and M. Osborne.

[iii] McKinsey, "Interim Report on Automation of Jobs", November 2015.

[iv] M. Arntz, T. Gregory and U. Zierahn (2016), "The Risk of Automation for Jobs in OECD Countries: A Comparative Analysis", OECD Social, Employment and Migration Working Papers, No. 189, OECD Publishing, Paris.

[v] https://www.therobotreport.com/news/amazon-has-30000-kiva-robots-at-work-alternatives-begin-to-compete

[vi] http://time.com/4458507/otto-uber-deal-driverless-autonomous-trucks/

[vii] Robert Solow, *New York Review of Books*, July 1987

[viii] https://www.gpo.gov/fdsys/pkg/ERP-2015

[ix] http://www.bls.gov/careeroutlook/2016/article/what-is-the-gig-economy.htm

The Enterprise Path to AI

Kimberly Powell, Senior Director of AI and Deep Learning, NVIDIA

As Senior Director of AI and Deep Learning at NVIDIA, Kimberly leads a global team that has blanketed the entire AI ecosystem from academia to start-ups to industry. The team's mission is to help researchers, engineers, and data scientists leverage transformative technology to make the impossible now possible in research and her team helps industries create new products and services powered by deep learning.

Prior to joining NVIDIA, Kimberly was a Product Manager for diagnostic imaging display systems at Planar Systems and was a Hardware Engineer at DOME Imaging Systems doing FPGA design. A graduate of Northeastern University, Kimberly holds a Bachelor of Science in Electrical Engineering with a concentration in Computer Engineering.

Artificial intelligence is changing our world. We experience it every day when we search the web, organize our photos, look at product recommendations and use our smartphones. These consumer applications are just the tip of the iceberg. Wide swaths of industries are in the midst of transformation.

In healthcare, for example, AI promises to alleviate the world's shortage of clinical staff through access to patient information, leading to more accurate diagnoses and personalized treatment plans. In transportation, Level 4 autonomous vehicles are expected on the roads in 2020.

Other industries – retail, manufacturing, financial services – are also in transition, benefiting from existing Big Data strategies that can now be fully realized with the power and application of AI. Critical business functions such as logistics, advertising, security, forecasting, site planning and product development will be improved and streamlined in the AI era by those enterprises who get on board quickly.

AI pioneer Andrew Ng recently declared: "AI is the new electricity. Electricity transformed countless industries; AI will now do the same."[i] Over the next three to five years, we predict that nearly every company in the world will be on their journey toward becoming an 'AI enterprise', in much the same way companies began the inevitable march to electrification in the late 19th century.

Surging interest in AI and business

AI is the ultimate computing challenge. Its fastest-growing segment – deep learning – has been fueled by the unprecedented power of the graphics processing unit (GPU), which delivers speed and accuracy. By training massive data sets with GPUs, and then putting those insights into action, enterprises can quickly tackle business challenges that were previously unsolvable.

During the past 24 months, my team and I have had discussions with hundreds of leaders at Fortune 500 companies and other enterprises. We have seen first-hand the surging interest in AI and how to apply it to critical business initiatives at the core of the enterprise, in order to gain competitive advantage.

By and large, today's AI adopters are found at two ends of the spectrum. On one end are tech giants like Google, Baidu, Facebook, Microsoft, Amazon and IBM, who are doubling down on AI. A recent Fortune article noted that Google had two deep-learning projects underway in 2012.[ii] Today, the company is pursuing more than 1000 projects across its major product sectors. Baidu, the Chinese search engine, uses AI to field customer questions and is testing an employee entry system based on face recognition at its headquarters in Beijing.

On the other end are a flurry of nimble, fast-moving start-ups. AngelList, an industry website, lists approximately 2000 AI start-ups and 2400 AI investors. CB Insights reports that funding for AI start-ups reached more than one billion dollars in 2016.[iii] While some have been acquired (for technology or talent or both), many remain independent.

Start-ups: agile, innovative, attractive

We believe AI start-ups will be a dominant force in driving AI progress over the next decade because of their 1) agility; 2) innovation mindset; 3) attractiveness to top AI researchers and developers. For organizations just starting to dip their toes in AI, partnering with a start-up offers an excellent way to begin the journey toward becoming an AI enterprise.

Below is an example of how an established digital media organization, MRM//McCann, successfully partnered with an AI start-up, Clarifai, to create an innovative AI-based advertising solution.

Case Study: AI and Advertising

Background: Clarifai is a young AI company that excels at visual recognition. Founded by Matthew Zeiler, Clarifai won the top five places in image classification at the ImageNet 2013 competition. The company makes its AI tools available in the form of application program interfaces (APIs) that start off as easy-to-implement lines of code, geared toward first-time developers or programmers, to more in-depth tools that allow greater levels of customization.

Challenge: MRM//McCann is a global digital marketing agency with offices in 22 countries. A client, Vattenfall, one of Europe's largest energy companies, desired an online 'contextual relevance' solution that would enable them to show potential customers the right product in real time. Contextual relevance is key to standing out amid the vast range of products being advertised online at every second.

Solution: MRM//McCann crafted a powerful ad platform for Vattenfall by enabling them to connect buyers with products based on the buyers' current online behavior. Clarifai's visual recognition solution enabled Vattenfall to 'see' the visual content that a potential customer was browsing on other sites and serve hyper-relevant display ads in real time. For example, if a website visitor was looking at photos of swimming pools, Vattenfall served an ad for a water temperature checker app next to the image. Through Clarifai, MRM//McCann was able to 'understand' millions of images and use that information to improve ad targeting, relevance and click-through.

The role of AI: Clarifai's technology uses AI to teach computers how to see. Visual recognition built on AI allows businesses to understand orders of magnitude more visual content – at the level of human accuracy or better – and use those insights to solve real-world problems. Clarifai's AI technology is particularly powerful because the algorithm gets 'smarter' with each use. For example, the more apples it sees, the better it becomes at identifying apples.

Getting started: the four Ps

To help companies get started, we recommend that they consider the four Ps: Perspective, People, Proof of Concept and Partners.

Perspective

Start reading! There is an abundance of information, advice and case studies online. Attend AI conferences, such as the International Conference on Machine Learning, the GPU Technology Conference and The AI Summit. Identify key opinion leaders in government. Host an AI speaker or meet-up at your company.

People

Identify your AI Person in Charge (PIC). Appoint an AI leadership team. Retrain and develop your teams by leveraging online AI courses from Udacity, Coursera and NVIDIA's Deep Learning Institute. Recruit from academia as well as industry.

Proof of concept

If you have not yet done so, we recommend that you launch an AI Proof of Concept (POC). Define a meaningful project that's important to growing revenue, improving operations, understanding consumer behavior or driving R&D. Challenge your teams (technical, marketing, ops) to work with an AI innovator.

Partners

You don't have to go it alone. Reach out to AI teams at companies like NVIDIA. Connect with start-ups. Introduce yourself to professors at local universities. Talk to GPU cloud platform providers, such as Microsoft, Amazon, Google and IBM. Explore open-source offerings, including AI frameworks such as TensorFlow, Caffe, Theano, Torch and others.

Finally, it's important to understand that AI is *very* data-centric. We advise companies to create a culture of 'data consciousness'. Many businesses are great at producing data, but they don't know what to do with it. They may even be throwing it away. If you don't yet have an AI initiative in place, build up rich data-sets that can help you in the future. *CIO* magazine advises: "Enterprise companies should refine their data analysis approach before they adopt AI-based systems. Data can be mined like a natural resource for insights that may lead to new concepts to test with users."[iv]

Conclusion

Computers now have the capacity to see, learn and react to complex situations as well as or better than humans. This is leading to a different way of thinking about products and services. Today's C-suite leaders have the opportunity to transform their organizations into AI enterprises that can compete successfully in the 21st century.

Clarifai's Matthew Zeiler says: "AI is a transformative technology that will become the new standard that every business must adapt to in order to stay competitive. Because of the exponential improvements in AI in a short period of time, it is imperative that businesses start thinking about their AI strategy today. Business leaders should be focused on choosing the best-in-class AI technology platforms they need to add to their AI stack."

How will you know when AI is working? Bryan Catanzaro, NVIDIA's head of applied AI research, puts it this way: "AI gets better and better until it kind of disappears into the background. Once you stop noticing that it's there because it works so well, that's when it's really landed."

i   https://www.techfutureslab.com/ai-machine-learning
ii   http://fortune.com/ai-artificial-intelligence-deep-machine-learning/
iii   https://www.cbinsights.com/blog/artificial-intelligence-startup-funding/
iv   http://www.cio.com/article/3125006/cloud-computing/the-state-of-artificial-intelligence-for-the-enterprise.html

When Artificial Intelligence is the Fastest Game in Town, Are You In or Out?

Jon Catling, Former Director, Global Data Architecture, Las Vegas Sands Corporation

---

Until recently Jon was responsible for developing the Data Strategy for Las Vegas Sands across the USA, Macau and Singapore, incorporating Data Management, Governance, and Data Science. His industry experience includes: Hospitality and Gaming, Geoscience, Exploration, Resource Mining, Building Materials Manufacturing, Banking/Insurance/Wealth Management, Agricultural Science, Software Development.

He is currently developing information management software, and a consulting framework for C-Level executive adoption and strategy of intelligence technology.

During 2016, I was stunned at the constant revelation of new and serious changes to the artificial intelligence (AI)/intelligent systems environments. At the point of writing this, the deluge of new applications is constant. Like a phase change to the state of matter, once enough energy has collected, suddenly everything changes. At AI Business' first AI Summit in London in May 2016, we saw the major players bring their toys out into the open in a concerted effort to show how much work had been going on. For them it has been some years in development, but for many it appeared as though a sudden explosion of new technology was miraculously appearing at our beck and call. Five months later, at The AI Summit San Francisco, the floodgates had opened and it seemed that everyone else was out and showing what they were doing. Since then, as I watch the reports flood in with each successive and successful conference, you get the feeling that this is one of the big ones. This is a phase change in technology.

Yet AI is not new. It's been around in ideas and fiction for generations. We have played with neural networks and interfaces and syntax for years and yet somehow, in 2015, we had Norvig and Chomsky arguing about analytics versus language and then a gush of tech to support the promise of a brave new world. Of course, like everything, the marketing approach is to give it a new paint job and pitch it as something brand new, even though the tech has been around for some time and for many of us there is no difference in the conceptual landscape. This is simply a natural progression. So why, then, am I so excited?

We still have to focus on data management and the progression of that data into information, except now the process is even more important. 'Garbage in, garbage out' for a BI report is a concern, yet it pales into insignificance if it's being used by an AI purchasing shares, or in conversation with a customer. Stuart Kauffmann, in his book *At Home in the Universe: The Search for Laws of Self-Organization and Complexity* (1995), posits that a complex adaptive system, as it grows, will develop emergent properties.[i] Properties not definable by the components of the system. I would suggest that the level of complexity with the community, taking into account technological adoption, social integration of the technology and the inherent maturity in the co-operative nature of integration, illustrated by Internet of Things (IoT), is at a point where the digital revolution, arguably building momentum since the 70s, will make a significant phase change, a flurry of acceptance by society, as it did with the smartphone. Meanwhile, the consequences are only just being considered by that same society. I remember being introduced to Alvin Toffler's *Future Shock* (1970) and *The Third Wave* (1980), and while Toffler barely mentions AI to any great degree, it is the evolution within the technology or digital revolution that formulates the change. In recent times I found myself inspired by Ray Kurzweil's *The Age of Intelligent Machines* (1990), *The Age of Spiritual Machines* (1999) and, appropriately, *The Singularity Is Near* (2006) that are most complementary with my own thinking. While the media abounds with commentary by all sorts of people weighing into the AI debate, much of the discussion is already available and suggests a way to humanistically adapt to it.

In the integrated resort, anything that impacts a customer's perception is critical. Managing that perception is everything. While you might be forgiven for categorizing Las Vegas Sands as part of the hospitality industry, our business model is somewhat unique. Everyone is used to staying at a hotel with a couple of bars, restaurants and shops, but the integrated resort is different, combining significant numbers of food and beverage outlets, shops, entertainment, conventions, as well as the gaming and hotel. This is a business model where the competition between domains is as rigorous as it is on The Strip. Couple that with resort guests that number in the thousands (tens of thousands during a convention) and this is not a place where you are likely to see robots trundling about; but it is a place where communication is critical.

If we define communications as "the expression or exchange of information or a means to express your ideas, thoughts, feelings, etc., to someone else", then the technology we use to effect that, to talk like that, to think like that, has to model itself on the person. Which means we are back to the Customer 360 model and are immediately confronted by its shortcomings. We need to get away from the multifaceted model. Instinctively, we create the model based on how each business domain sees the customer; while, in fact, it has to be about how the customer sees the business. The relationship between the domains is already fractured and simply reflecting that is pointless. The most useful deliverable is personalized data, applicable to the customer, not just to the domain.

Once we add AI into the recipe, we need to take the Customer 360 concept and transform it to the Customer DNA model, which has the ability to establish profile segments augmented by analytics, which are then rewrapped around the individual's personality model. This is the only objective that suits the business relationship with their customer. Finding a restaurant that suits your preference and taste and directing you to the toilet are equally important to the guest.

From my perspective, there is nothing new in all this. During the past five years, we have been adding to the traditional data management processes with master data, the variations of the ever-increasing 3Vs (volume, variety and velocity) of Big Data with the focus on providing three key capabilities: reporting, real-time and prediction services, aka the past, present, and future, so to speak. Our new model continues to focus on data science, preparation, transformation and analytics and now adds AIConcierge, and the chatbot (the 'new channel'). Now we talk about Big Data being the formula to create semantic ingestion for machine learning because the key and most critical success factor is to be competent with our ability to speak to the customer. If we get that right we are okay, because if we get that right we have time. Time to engage, time to make the right connection between our services and the potential customer experience.

It is the AIConcierge and the chatbot that is the key to applying the technology. The chatbot serves as a channel, a method that allows people to interact with business, and the AIConcierge, the intelligent system, serves to create a layer of interpretation and access to a greater amount of information than we can provide in the form of placing people on the floor, the call center or on the front desk. The capability of intelligent systems is to field information from a variety of sources and to be able to create opportunities and enhance relationships within the organization so that when a customer asks a question he/she can receive the best single answer at that one point in time.

In our Las Vegas properties, the Venetian and the Palazzo, we have over 7000 rooms and we are 90%+ full all the time. Last week, Amazon was using our convention center and the number of attendees was listed at approximately forty thousand. So, approximately 50,000 people milling around. Maintaining the best possible service can place extraordinary strains on the resources available. For those people who want coffee, it's a fairly simple thing; but for those who want to find out the location of a shop or a restaurant, staring through the crowd of 40,000 people that have just exited the convention rooms is overwhelming. The ability for us to enable some method of communication with a level of intelligence that we can respond to questions even at the simplest level is fundamental.

But the chatbot is just the channel; behind the scenes the intelligence system requirements are significant. In the first instance, we have to 'chat', and I am not talking about the standardized approach we are used to, the advertising on television which has somewhat translated itself to our web pages. We're not trying to blast you with everything; what we offer is to chat with you. We know that people like to chat, are willing to chat, but that chat needs to be a very human flow. In retrospect, the chat on smartphones has become a very natural way of communicating and the key to it is the syntax, the flow, the 'chit-chat', that people have adopted and we need to adopt.

And we are not trying to fool the guest. It is not about Turing's Test, because, honestly, humans anthropomorphize so often that we will simply accept the chatbot is alive, if not human. That issue will become a social one, where the ethics and behavior of the user is the focus. Just ask Microsoft's Cortana.

We can assume, we can predict, we can engage. In this case, what we're trying to do is to find a way of delivering precisely what you want almost as soon as you're thinking about it. Your behavior is indicative of a human being. And your behavior is habitual. But are you going to do it every time? In the same way as analytics is indicative, not precise, so we can establish a profile of the patterns of behavior customers assume as indicative. It is not about saying "this is what you will do." It is about saying "this is what you might; and so long as we don't start assuming precision, we will be in a better position to be able to respond to that." So here we have the intelligence system's ability to read, to interpret, to create relationships, to build on opportunities.

Is there ethics involved? You can bet your pants there is! However, both the consumers and the producers of these intelligent systems need to appreciate the value to them as well as the difference between personalization and Personalization. We don't create the model to predict behavior, but rather to enable the ability to change with that behavior. The approach here is to be able to respond to the situation rather than react to it. This is the key to the effective and ethical use of AI.

So there we have it. That is where we are now. The chatbot as a medium. Focused on 'chatting', engaging, and creating a relaxed conversation, the AIConcierge enables the exposure of information to build relationships between data points or go to components within an organization. And within the customer's behavior and organization. Analytics for ingestion and create the foundations of the intelligence. Then real-time events to articulate the live flow.

But wait, there's more!

This is what we need to be discussing and watching for, so that we can respond rather than react to the expanding technology; but we do need to learn from experience and to think things through thoroughly. Let's return to the idea of a Customer 360 model. It is intended to make us think beyond our individual perspective. Indeed, what I have described is the AIConcierge and chatbot for my view of the business model of the integrated resort.

But from the industry perspective, there are a couple of issues that are going to break the ongoing opportunities. What are you going to do when the number of chatbots that can connect to you starts to get out of control? Many people stay at many hotels, take holidays at many locations, use multiple sites for the same sort of activity, such as booking air tickets. All those chatbots with the ability to 'chat'. That new and seamless ability to communicate with you uncontrollably. Imagine that you have all these bots chatting, saying, "Hi, how are you going? ... Can I help you? ... Can I do anything for you? ..." It is going to become a source of irritation and you might begin to weigh the value of keeping the connection despite it being a source of value. I don't need to look at the website if I can ask what is available; but would it not be easier if I only had to talk to 'one' bot, one bot to rule them all?

Well, that technology is already in play. The Intelligent Personal Assistant (IPA), the personal interface to your Watson, Cortana, Alexa, Siri, et al. A personalized interface between you and all the activities that are happening in your world. Ask it to book meetings, research a weekend away, sync up with the kids' school calendars. Set the itinerary for your next business trip, and it chats to the bots/APIs and plans your tickets, appointments and accommodation. So far it's in the early stages of maturity and, like many systems, there are implications to using it. For example, fundamentally an AI learns. It is not so much rule-based as developing rules that support human behavior and we, the user, need to be a part of that.

Now consider for a moment the ability to create your own individual interface. That system has to figure out what it is you want and infer what is going to happen and needs to happen. Which leads us to the last feature I need to talk about. For the IPA to work effectively, it needs to learn about you specifically. It needs to understand your language syntax, your behavior, the patterns of your day-to-day activity. For this to happen, it will need to be not just 'always on'; instead, it will be 'always listening' and continuously ingesting and evaluating. Making connections and relationships between your texts, emails, conversations on and off the phone. At the end of a meeting you will find a list of actions to confirm, a summary of the conversation, PowerPoint, and a to-do list. In addition, a list of searches on the internet and internal content.

Always listening, always processing and evaluating. What happens when an external agency wants to get access to that information? What happens to the data, and who owns it? The new breed of chipsets that are aimed at AI in processing capabilities and while the data may continue to be in the cloud the processing and learning needs to be an extension of your own personal space. For me, the possibilities are endless. I see AI systems keeping an eye on the elderly or infirmed, or as an extension of education systems. If they are managed effectively, they enable, not exclude; but that does not mean people won't take opportunities that are not to humanity's benefit. I apologize to the commercial players: I can't wait for your IPAs in the making – I am developing my own. This is too exciting. Too emergent. A phase change, and it's happening right now.

---

[i]   Stuart Kauffmann, *At Home in the Universe: The Search for Laws of Self-Organization and Complexity*; Oxford University Press Inc.; New e. edition (6 Feb. 1997)

The Rebirth of the Financial Industry

**Kumar Srivastava, VP, Products & Strategy,
BNY Mellon**

────────────────

Kumar Srivastava has spent his career building Big Data, analytics, machine learning, API and app products as part of a diverse and broad area set such as social networking, online security, identity, reputation and trust management, online fraud and abuse, online search and advertising, digital platforms, mobile applications and monetization services.

Kumar has worked with organizations of all sizes, from Fortune 50 companies to midsize businesses and small start-ups, and he has been involved in research at Columbia University and has led products that have been honored as industry-defining by customers and analysts. He has been published in Forbes, Wired, Entrepreneur, Bloomberg and other publications and has authored two books on the subjects of Digital Transformations and API Product Management. (His views are personal and do not reflect those of BNY Mellon).

The future is cut-throat and harsh

Like almost every other vertical, the world of finance is ripe for disruption through the application of artificial intelligence (AI) and machine learning (ML) in how, what and when business is done. The financial industry is already being and will continue to be disrupted by digitization, automation and disintermediation. However, the impact of AI, ML and natural language processing (NLP) will be immense and irreversible.

The financial industry: A decade from now

Technology ceases to be an advantage

In the future, moats developed by enterprises through the early adoption of technology will be eroded. Early-mover advantages will cease to protect enterprises and enable them to continue offering a differentiated proposition. Technology will be widely adopted across the industry and thus would cease to provide an advantage and instead will become a common characteristic of all incumbents. At the same time, with the advent and adoption of open-source software, all enterprises will essentially have free access to high-quality building blocks.

Open-source software will be the great equalizer in all industries, including the financial industry, and this growth will fundamentally reshape what and how software is written within an enterprise. At the same time, enterprises that refuse to keep up with the pace of technology adoption will quickly become known as laggards and these shortcomings will be easily visible in not only their products and service offerings, but also in the quality of service and satisfaction that they provide to their clients and users.

Client experience becomes table stakes

Clients, users and customers will become accustomed to high levels of interesting, intelligent products and services. They will expect products and services that understand them, their current state, their current values and their future desired state and values. Users will expect the products and services from their service providers to adapt, adjust and improve to ensure that the users are able to achieve their desired financial state with minimal effort, risk and cost.

On the flip side, products that do not offer such an experience will be quickly weeded out, abandoned *en masse* and distinctively called out for lack of empathy. Given the software-driven nature of products and services (as we are seeing with the growth of fintechs), the barrier to entry to the financial industry will be greatly reduced, eventually offering clients and customers an incredible choice of software-driven products and services. At that point, client experience will be the differentiating and deciding factor in customer acquisition and retention.

In addition, the software-driven nature of products and services (as evident from current changes such as PSD2) will sharply reduce switching costs for users and clients between different financial service providers. This reduction in switching cost will drive the focus on client experience, satisfaction and value.

Clients and users will expect high levels of quality of service across the board, be it responsiveness of the service provider, transparency and visibility into the processing and servicing of the client needs, security and an abuse- and fraud-free experience and service delivered within the required time and accuracy guidelines and SLAs.

Basic investment strategies become table stakes

With a common layer of software driving a very similar-looking product and service-offering landscape regardless of the service provider, the basic levels of services are likely to be indistinguishable from each other. This means that service providers will need to create new offerings that offer higher-levels of value; offerings that are customized to each client and provable as high-performing and consistently delivering value. In addition, clients will demand new market-building offerings that generate new opportunities for clients and, at the same time, reduce the cost, complexity and risk for the clients to leverage these opportunities. On the other hand, entry-level investment strategies will offer no differentiation and will often be relegated to low-cost offerings.

Agility is not a choice

The rise of the fintechs will cease to be just a trend, but will become commonplace, with fintechs offering agility as a service to financial service providers, enabling them to bring new products and services to market faster, with lower risk and cost. Fintechs will offer new value across smarter and more intelligent infrastructure, platform and applications. Incumbents will embrace fintechs as a necessary agility boost and fintechs will see incumbents as shorter, faster paths to market. As these working models evolve and mature, clients and users will be greeted with new, better products faster with higher quality and, at the same time, products that iterate and improve faster and more efficiently. Clients will expect agility from service providers and the lack of such agility will become a roadblock to client satisfaction as it begins to block innovation and value generation for the client.

Things that don't change

Regulation and audit

The financial industry is susceptible to changing regulatory and audit constraints. The requirement to remain compliant, responsive to regulatory needs and changes in policy while ensuring that regulators have the ability to access data required to regulate the market as a whole will continue to pose challenges to enterprises in the financial industry.

Recent political turmoil is proof that levels and types of regulation requirements imposed on the financial industry will be continually shifting and morphing. Even though regulations might increase or decrease in number or complexity, or both, financial enterprise will be in need of insulating themselves from such changes through automation and proactive risk identification and mitigation. The entire industry will see an increase in investments to add more intelligence and proactive mechanisms to detect and react to risk.

Fraud

Given the high-value transactions and amount of capital involved, the financial industry has always been and will continue to be a target for financial fraud. Regulations such as Know Your Customer (KYC) and Anti-Money Laundering (AML) continue to be required, given the propensity for fraud to be carried out. Being able to detect fraud swiftly and accurately will continue to be a very high priority for financial companies.

Fraud is and will continue to shift from insider attacks to newly opened vectors enabled through the digitization of all customer-product interfaces and touch points. The perils faced by consumer online services will bleed into financial services and products, leading to an increase in fraud and malicious impersonation and account takeovers. The financial services industry will need to quickly react and not only assimilate the technology perfected at consumer-focused companies, but participate in preparing the defenses for the next generation of attacks of fraud and malice.

Risk and complexity

The financial industry tends to be very complex at the macro level and large financial enterprises tend to be fairly complex, with many different relationships, dealings, products and services. This complexity can lead to blind spots, silos and hidden risks. Detecting and removing any such risk that can strike any time continues to be of high priority to financial companies.

With increasing complexity and the introduction of new product and service workflows and more signals that can be captured, monitoring and tracking known risk vectors and identifying newly created risk and complexity from shifting client segments, market conditions and product/services will require superhuman capability, essentially transforming the function from manual or hybrid manual/automatic capabilities to fully automated, constantly churning intelligence. Ability to identify and mitigate risk will become a competitive advantage and will be a major contributor to enterprise longevity.

Enter AI

The future of the financial industry will be completely submerged in AI-driven products, services, interfaces and experiences. AI will permeate its way through the financial services industry within and across various service providers. It will govern how products and services are designed, built, delivered to clients and supported. The entire product lifecycle will be reshaped through the application of AI.

Artificial intelligence will lead to the birth of a new generation of infrastructure, platforms and applications, with key core capabilities replaced or augmented by AI.

Product and service design

Product and service design will get a boost from the ability of AI to generate and detect micro segments of users and activity and devise products, features and experiences to target these segments with highly customized offerings. AI-driven systems, coupled with across-the-board digitization, will have the ability to process any and all data generated and find hidden patterns and signals that specify high business risk or high business value.

Changing user demographics

Millennials are already showing distrust in financial advisors that take large fractions of the investment capital in return for investment advice and money management. At the same time, the complexity of the financial markets has made millennials averse to entering the them. Either hampered by lack of financial knowledge or restricted by funds required to invest, millennials exhibit low levels of interest. This poses a long-term risk to the financial industry, as it means millennials graduate into the most financially lucrative segment of users. In this situation, financial firms have to not only reduce the cost of providing advising and money management services, but also reduce the complexity in the financial instruments they offer to their users. Artificial intelligence and ML have the potential to provide smart assistants, smart advisors, and intelligent interfaces that understand and predict products and services that best fit the needs of their clients and deliver those services at a fraction of the cost, as complex systems and teams of employees required to run these products and services are either no longer required or get greatly simplified with much higher efficiencies.

However, more importantly, AI-driven technologies will offer the ability to target specific millennials with custom-crafted and designed service offerings delivered with and through an experience customized and personalized for each individual user. AI will enable the identification and delivery of customized experiences and messaging to individual users given their current context of time, location, channel of product usage, point and stages in their lives, workflows and environment.

Risk management

Given the increased digitization of financial products and services, the future will be fraught with an increase in activity, interactions and transactions running through a complex ecosystem with multiple service providers. To protect clients, service providers will need to look beyond just their systems or their products and services to the ecosystems to which they belong. Risk detection and management needs to happen at the ecosystem level and thus will require super-intelligent systems that are able to detect risk at the macro level with the ability to transcend organization boundaries.

Artificial intelligence and ML will offer the ability to build rich risk management systems through anomaly detection, behavior profiling and pattern matching. These capabilities offer superhuman ability to inspect data and information from across the financial stack, recognize patterns of expected and unexpected behavior and generate alerts, warnings, and recommendations to enable the firm to adjust to, adapt, and anticipate risk. Better understanding of clients, their behavior, fraud, anti-money laundering, and risky and anomalous activity at both a macro and micro level will secure the market, protect the clients and service providers, thereby reducing the operating costs. This, in turn, benefits the clients through higher levels of service, with more satisfaction delivered at lower costs.

Predicting client behavior

Artificial intelligence and ML will have a significant impact on predicting client behavior that enables the financial industry and its constituent firms to predict their clients' needs and adjust their services to provide the best in class service. Clients typically have well-defined goals and strategies that determine their financial activities for buying, selling, trading and money operations. AI and ML have the ability to generate an entire new class of services that find the shortest, most cost-efficient and risk-averse path to meeting those goals and objectives. For example, consider a financial product custom-designed for a newly graduated student in their first job that factors in their student loans and generates a strategy that enables the student to pay off their loan while providing a long-term payoff.

In addition, AI and ML will enable firms to provide personalized and customized services to their firms, thereby generating higher levels of satisfaction and value for the clients. In parallel, cross-client behavior analysis through sophisticated pattern detection has the ability to highlight and uncover hidden risk in the market, for segments of clients or for the firm itself. High quality AI and ML will have the ability to provide a risk management-driven competitive advantage to firms that move to invest in these technologies.

Being able to predict client behavior offers the following opportunities. AI and ML, when used to profile the investment behavior of a client, can be used to proactively suggest, recommend and enable such strategies for the client. This reduces work and effort required for the client to produce the outcomes of the investment strategy they desire.

The ability to predict client behavior is also fodder for detecting unusual behavior and patterns when clients do not perform activities that the system predicts the client will perform. When such occurrences happen, the service provider can proactively reach out to the client to determine whether these are intended or unintended changes.

Another example of AI-driven intelligent service offerings is the ability to optimize service offerings and their internal processing workflows based on the wholesale, across-the-board predicted patterns of types and volumes of client requests. Service providers will be able to use AI to organize themselves to be more efficient and produce a higher quality of service levels with lower cost and more predictable returns.

At the same time, client activity and how it is processed within the service provider and its ultimate outcome (success or failure) can be used to determine predictive models that describe when certain client activity will end up in an error, causing client dissatisfaction and loss of value. These predictive models can be used to quickly recover from client-facing errors or even used to prevent such errors from happening, leading to a better and more satisfactory client experience.

Conclusion

The impact of AI and ML will increase exponentially in the financial industry. Firms will look to the tech industry to lead the way in the generation and adoption of AI and ML to various scenarios that are common to and relevant to the financial industry. The financial industry will be able to leverage AI and ML technologies that are available in open-source to quickly ramp up and build out these capabilities in-house. At the same time, the number of vendors offering such capabilities will also increase several-fold. The financial industry will be severely changed and impacted by AI and ML, and incumbents that are left standing or are resistant to adopting these technologies will have a tough future ahead. At the same time, firms that begin their AI and ML journey sooner than others will build a moat of competitive advantage that will serve them well in the coming decades.

Creating Digital Assistants

Noel Lyons, Director of Digital Design, Barclays

Noel Lyons heads up Barclays' Digital Design team, focused on creating beautiful and useful digital experiences for millions of customers. Noel was previously Founding partner of London-based award-winning design agency KentLyons. He has previously worked with BSS and the BBC; Noel produced the first proof copies of Harry Potter and the Philosopher's Stone, by a then-unknown J.K. Rowling during his time at Bloomsbury Publishing.

How we're designing with AI tools to help our customers

We've been developing digital assistants to help our customers manage their financial lives. And we've been combining AI technologies and human-centered design practices to do it. Here's a quick overview of what we've done so far, what we've learnt, and where we're headed next.

Helping people achieve their ambitions

Barclays is a massive organization, as I found out when I joined. We have 100,000 colleagues, working around the globe. And in the UK alone, we have a huge customer base. Our CEO likes to make the point that 24m people interact with our services in the UK. That's one out of every two adults in the UK. So it's essential that we're always thinking about our customers. Our aim is clear too – we're focused on helping people achieve their ambitions. That ambition can be many things. To buy a house or plan for a comfortable retirement. Or just to be able to check your account without getting stressed. At the root of this mission is the idea of connecting people and money.

Making banking completely personalized

We want to make the experience of banking completely personalized, which is where AI comes in. We want to be your financial partner, helping you understand your money, predict the future and work in sync with you. We want to be proactive and reactive. Looking at the data that makes up your financial life and giving you the insights you need. And we want to tailor this to everyone's unique circumstances. As a company, we're data-rich. Banking transactions are just data points. Using AI and machine learning, we can interpret this data to help empower our customers. But there is so much data. The question we're facing now is – what should we focus on? What will AI be good for, and what will it augment from our existing services?

Solving human problems and answering core human needs

This is where design comes in. Design is at root of the business of solving human problems and answering core human needs. By applying human-centered design, we can focus on what is most important to customers. Where their pain points are, where the friction is. And this isn't a case of us asking people what they want.

We're not trying to make a faster horse

Henry Ford said if he'd asked people what they wanted, they would have said they wanted a faster horse. Human-centered design is not about asking people what they want. It's not about trying to make a faster horse. It's more akin to a doctor. We don't ask "what do you want?" Instead, we ask "Where does it hurt?" We do this in many ways. We do copious research. We analyze reams of data and analytics. We run regular diary studies. We build rapid prototypes and test with real customers. We test and tweak and iterate and retest constantly. This isn't because we're nervous or lacking in confidence, but because we're trying to get closer to the pain of our customers. And we've identified some clear, powerful user needs. One stands out for me.

How can we help people be better off?

As a bank, we should be able to achieve this. We're good with numbers, we're the experts when it comes to money. And, all our research tells us that our customers are desperate for this. It comes right back to our core mission – helping people achieve their ambition. Better-off can come in many ways. From small things like letting people know when they've gone overdrawn, to big things like planning for their retirement. But how can we do this – how can we help people be better-off? And how can we use AI tools to achieve this? Furthermore, how can those AI tools work with our branch and call center colleagues to remove some of the admin so they can provide the real empathy and human service that our customers want and need? We started by looking around for a comparable model outside of banking.

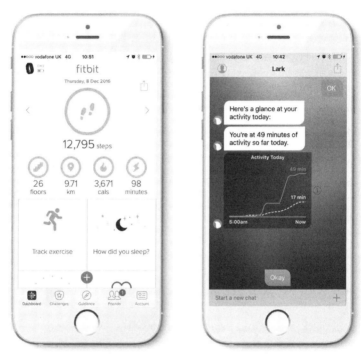

Figure 1: Health apps help us track our progress as we improve our physical fitness. But what about financial fitness? (Credit: Barclays)

Luckily, there's a huge offering around this in the area of physical health (see Figure 1). There's a wealth of apps in this space, focused on trying to help you get fitter, get healthier, improve your lifestyle and achieve your fitness goals.

We learnt a few things from these health apps, and our experiments with them. We can alert people and remind them about their financial health. We can give them information about how to run their finances. We can nudge them in the right direction. We can present personalized information about their performance. We can listen and react.

Design sprints and demos

So we created a very rapid prototype of what the service might look like, and tested it with real customers. We built a decision tree engine which allowed us to structure conversations with our customers. We used a conversational interface so we could make it feel like a genuine assistant. And we used a series of buttons that allowed the user to respond to the questions easily. We'd previously experimented with NLP and intent training for full AI agents, but the process at the time was lengthy, and the training process was complex. But the worst outcome was that the user interface was frustrating – you had to work out the right questions to ask before you got a sensible response.

When we initially experimented with NLP-only interfaces, the whole experience failed, and felt effortful. By limiting ourselves and our users to preformatted responses, we could take the effort out but still have a conversation. At first, we experimented with the concept of a finance coach. An assistant that gives you insight into your spending habits, your recent activity, spend categorization, and tips about how you could improve your financial health. We tested and iterated the prototype over four weeks, testing each week. We then explored it with larger groups to see the reaction people had to the experience. And we discovered that people were desperate for this sort of service. They loved it. About one third of people wanted to be able to write their own questions and have more than just buttons, but they reported it was a minor frustration. The rest of our testers didn't even notice they couldn't write their own questions. They just didn't need to.

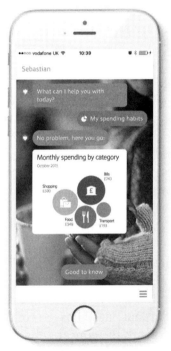

Figure 2: A digital assistant that helps you manage your money (Credit: Barclays)

One thing that became clear with designing a digital assistant is that we were designing a relationship over time. Normally, when we design an experience we're designing in space. We map out the flow, and we make it as painless as possible for users to travel through this flow. But here, the flow was completely dependent on the customer information, choices, and triggers. We're designing services that would reintroduce themselves into people's lives at pertinent moments.

Figure 3: Creating conversations allows us to design over time (Credit: Barclays)

Here's an example. We point out that it's payday. We've managed to assess that it is payday, and not just an influx of money, either through some clever algorithm, or we just ask users. We send an alert. And then, we change the design slightly – we have a nice, happy picture, because it's payday. And we give the user some helpful information – they had money left in their account on payday. This gives us the perfect opportunity to talk about payday saving. Behavioral economics tells us that the best time to talk to someone about saving is on payday, when they have money. The worst time is a week before payday, when they're just trying to stay in the black. So we give some insight about it, and then

Figure 4: Assistant in Launchpad (Credit: Barclays)

help them set it up. In a few weeks' time, we can contact them again about some other element of their finances. But the triggers are based on their personalized information, and we can score the triggers to ensure relevancy and importance to the user.

We've introduced the digital assistant to Launchpad to see what people make of it.

We've had some interesting feedback so far. Firstly, people love it as an idea. All ages get the idea, and especially with older, more traditional customers, we get some great

Figure 5: Unlock Britain app (Credit: Barclays)

feedback. One user, who was 75, an ex-miner, who doesn't bank online but does use his phone to message his kids and grandkids, was able to make payments faster than using the normal in-app method. But his comments were telling. He said the regular payment journey through the app meant you were the customer *and* the cashier. But this brought the cashier back. It actually feels like we're trying to help.

And this relationship people have with humans is critical. Our next experiment was our Unlock Britain app. We designed this for users overseas either visiting or living in the UK or looking to invest in the UK. Usually, our relationship managers either in-branch or in call centers help these customers work through things like education or buying property in the UK. But that often meant our highly talented staff were stuck processing basic information. What if we could digitize this interaction? So we could answer the initial questions users had, but in the same friendly, human way they would with a colleague in-branch? Again, using a decision tree engine and a button-driven conversational interface, we created an easy-to-use, information-rich service that qualified interested customers. It allowed them to speak to the right people, and provide them with a great level of service.

What have we learned?

Users love it – but it needs to do more

On first contact, users enjoy using it. But they quickly learn its limitations. And this is likely to be a problem for AI solutions for a while – as inquisitive humans, we try to find the limits, the boundaries. And maybe that's because we want it to be really clever and powerful. Or perhaps because we'd rather it wasn't...

But our users, especially older users who are more used to a regular in-branch relationship, find this sort of interaction really useful. It's a great way to introduce an older-user base to a new format. And that's because everyone can text, everyone can talk, and the interface isn't alienating or confusing. There is very little to learn by way of tools.

And there are some clear accessibility benefits here too. By using interfaces that are familiar and very easy to grasp, we make using our services better for everyone. This isn't just about providing for people with specific access issues – it's about making the services we provide easier to use across the board. At Barclays, we believe accessibility has a beneficial effect for all users. So we'll continue to test with a broad audience, with different levels of skills and experience to ensure we can take everyone with us. By thinking of edge cases and those who might get left behind, we believe we'll create services that are better for all users.

NLP and intent engines are great when they work, but frustrating when they don't

Thus far, NLP tools need either a greater degree of training, or they need to get better at inferring. Currently, our experiments with them have meant that we've avoided using them. We'll get there, for sure, but the button-based decision tree interface, despite its limitations, is less annoying and disruptive for our users than trying to guess how to ask the right question.

Deep AI is not required yet – decision trees can work well as a proxy

We haven't yet come across a need for something *really* clever. We can plot out most of the customer needs and things they want to access, so we can map successful paths to the right end result. It's possible that, as we grow in capability, we'll need a more autonomous, flexible, intelligent system. If we really want to partner with our customers, and be a vital part of their lives, we're going to have to get there. But at these early stages, it's not essential.

Tone of voice is crucial – we need to get permission in order to make it feel okay

We believe it's fundamental to ask permission from the outset. A bot trawling through your account and presenting insights can feel intrusive. So it's crucial that we ask "Is this okay?" Even though we already have all this information to hand, and our customers know we do, the act of asking permission is really important. It says clearly that this is their information, and we get to look at it and interrogate it only with their say-so. Our customers are in charge.

It can free up branch and call center colleagues to add real help

By taking away some of the low-level form-filling and simpler activities, we hope this can free up our teams in branch and in call centers to add real value to people. This isn't a replacement to human interactions – it should be an enabler. There is, quite rightly, a lot of concern around how AI technology will make jobs redundant. We've seen this before with other levels of automation throughout industrial and technological developments, and the fear is often overstated. Barclays has experience in this – we launched the first ATM, the first credit card in the UK, were quick to launch online banking, and were first to market with our mobile app and ideas like Pingit. And yet we have more employees now than ever before. And we're delivering a better service than ever before too. We know that these advances are great at handling things that can be automated. And they free up our in-branch and on-call colleagues to do what humans are innately good at – empathy, reasoning, problem-solving.

We've also looked at how we can deliver a seamless handover from AI to human interaction. We want our digital assistant to be humane, but not human. It doesn't have a name, or an avatar, and that's deliberate. That way, when we hand over to a human colleague to take over a conversation, we can announce it clearly: "I'm handing you over to Jes now. But, unlike me, Jes is a real person, so please be nice."

Proactive and reactive

The key thing people really want and respond well to is when we're proactively monitoring their account with them. When we're pointing out how we might help save them money, or make more money, or avoid charges. And when something changes, or is about to change, we react appropriately. If they tell us they don't want to hear from us so much, we quiet down. If they're checking their account more regularly, we offer to automate the checking process. The key is to be monitoring and assessing all the time, always on, to create a reliable, meaningful digital assistant. And it's by employing the oceans of data we already have, unique to us as a bank with often life-long relationships with our customers, that we can help our customers predict and anticipate. By doing that we can again reduce the friction, ease the pain and partner effectively with our customers' lives.

We're just starting, and there's a lot more to come, but we know that being proactive and reactive is the way forward, as our customers really appreciate it.

Where next?

This is a huge space and we're growing our capabilities all the time.

Voice

We are, like everyone else, looking at voice-driven interfaces. Whether this becomes the new normal, or if it remains just an additional way of accessing information, remains to be seen. But the accessibility use case is clear, and we're focused on being as accessible to all as we can. Voice interfaces can provide that greater level of accessibility, and we're experimenting to deliver this.

Other channels and platforms

We want to be where our customers are. Which means we need to look at how we can be useful on other platforms. We're interested in how we work with large platforms such as Facebook, Whatsapp, Skype and others to be there for our customers.

Increasing assistant features based on customer needs

Whatever we do next, it's vital that we continue to focus heavily on our customer needs: what is going to add the most value for them, and will lead to a demonstrably better experience.

It's an everchanging, growing area, and we're pushing hard. And we want to be part of the discussion around AI and design, how it will affect our lives and how it should be used. We're figuring out the answers to this by designing and trialling with our customers, to ensure we've got their interests at heart. And we are being open about our work so we can engage in the conversations about this technology. We don't have all the answers, and we're finding our way by *doing*. We'd love to hear from anyone else doing the same so we can share learnings and best practice in order to deliver better, easier, more personalized services for our customers.

Take Cover! How AI Will Upend Insurance, and Why that Matters for Us All

Simeon Preston, Group COO, AIA Group

Simeon Preston is AIA's Group Chief Operations Officer and a member of the Group Executive Committee. He is responsible at the Group level for operations, technology and innovation. He is a director of various companies within the Group. He joined the Group in September 2010 and is based in Hong Kong. Prior to joining the Group, Mr. Preston served as a senior partner in the financial services practice of global management consultants Bain & Company, where he specialized in the Asia life insurance sector. He previously spent almost nine years with strategy consulting firm Marakon Associates in Europe, the US and Asia, and was named a partner in 2006.

Mr. Preston holds an MBA with distinction from INSEAD in France and Master of Science degrees from the University of Newcastle upon Tyne and Leicester University in the UK. He also holds a BSc from the London School of Economics.

Artificial intelligence (AI) will be extensively adopted in insurance, and the industry will experience radical change as a result. All the major disciplines under the AI banner – natural language processing, machine learning, deep learning, image interpretation, optical character recognition and others – have readily available and broad-reaching application across most types of insurance. The question is no longer whether AI will change the game, but where and how this will happen, and how fast.

If the underpinning of AI effectiveness is data, the insurance industry is ripe for the taking. As the custodians of vast amounts of customer information accumulated over many years and territories, insurers have long used advanced analytics to manage risk, optimize operations, understand clients' needs and arm salespeople with leads. To permit these and other kinds of data analysis, insurers had to structure and organize their information as best they could. This was the beginning of the AI journey for many insurers and has helped them prepare for the AI renaissance now taking shape.

These data-organizing activities have only gone so far. Artificial intelligence applications in insurance have historically been constrained by challenges with data quality. Many insurers with consumers as clients still hold the majority of their document records in flat-file scanned images, and some still own vast warehouses of paper. This was due in equal part to regulatory requirements (for wet signatures, say), storage limitations inherent in ageing policy administration systems, and a reliance on legacy manual processes for underwriting, policyholder servicing and claims management. While most insurers' finance and actuarial systems were modernized and automated a long time ago, too often their other operations have lagged behind.

The relatively recent rise of the internet, social networks and smart devices has permitted the collection of vast new pools of data, and opened up entirely new ways for insurers to interact with their customers. The rising use of digital tools and the modernization of new policy administration systems permits far richer data to be collected, which can be organized and manipulated efficiently using the storage, processing power and network bandwidth now widely available at low marginal cost. Paper-based application forms are now giving way to tablet-based interactive sales tools that permit online delivery of financial needs analysis, real-time quotations, automated underwriting, electronic signature, premium payment and policy issuance. As each of these steps is automated, so the breadth, quality, and accessibility of data expand. This in turn permits the application of AI tools in each step of the insurance value chain.

Irrespective of who they are or what protection they hold, all insurance customers go through four fundamental experience steps: learn, buy, service, and claim. To learn about insurance, customers increasingly do their own research online before they speak to an advisor: more than 60% of individual purchasers in Asia first use a search engine to understand their insurance needs and choices. To buy life and health insurance, most consumers prefer to seek expert advice before paying their first premium: less than 2% of policies in Asia are currently bought online, although ever more personal lines (motor, home, travel, and so forth) are being bought or renewed direct. Policyholders have many ways to service their policy – through their advisor, call center, walk-in branch or online – and many are moving toward digital self-service. To submit a claim, most still revert to paper-based documentation given the need for verification of loss and/or payment, though claims automation is emerging rapidly here too.

AI will increasingly touch each of these four customer experience steps in profound though differing ways.

Step 1: Learn

Insurance customers today increasingly do their research online before they speak to the advisors about their needs. Rather than calling their broker, web searches and company websites are increasingly where customers go first to find the information they need. Whilst information on websites has typically been static and incomplete, online chatbots trained through AI to answer consumers' most frequent queries are becoming a common feature in financial services of all kinds. Want to know more about a particular product? What is the difference between plan A and plan B? If I am a single working woman aged 28, which life insurance product is bought by people like me? Chatbots are being trained to answer these questions using natural language dialogues purged of insurance jargon. They will become the first line of advice to many customers seeking immediate responses-to-queries access to information they cannot find elsewhere.

Step 2: Buy

The deployment of robo-advisors (a misnomer: they are algorithms, not real robots) to augment and support relationship managers will transform productivity during the consultation and sales process. These online platforms, generating automated advice based on algorithms without the need for any human invention, are being deployed widely in private banking, and insurance will quickly follow. The underlying machine learning tools will process large amounts of data to predict and anticipate needs. They will guide customers to seemingly bespoke solutions and provide unbiased advice and product recommendations. If configured correctly, these tools can also provide an audit trail of decision support to strengthen insurers' sales compliance. Robo-advisors may well not supplant the role of a human advisor for life and health insurance, where personal contact and human empathy are intrinsic to the consultation process. They will instead allow human advisors to deepen their customer relationships and give better-quality advice, and free up capacity so they can focus on the most valuable client interactions.

Most insurance underwriting involves repeated rules-based decision-making with an element of expert judgment borne of experience. As such, it is ripe for modernization using machine learning. Routine new business applications can be processed automatically by algorithms that assess and classify risks based on a full history of past decisions and experience. This will yield faster decisions on risk and pricing to most applicants, whilst freeing up the most experienced human underwriters to focus on highly complex and first-of-a-kind cases.

Product pricing will undergo its own transformation as a result of machine learning. Motor insurance premiums are already being adjusted based on driving behavior, as rated using algorithms processing data from GPS, telemetry and in-vehicle accelerometers. In the near future, some motor insurers will gamify the driving experience to encourage customers to compete against their peers for 'good driving' rewards. Whilst more complex to design, similar techniques may ultimately be applicable in life, health and other types of protection.

Step 3: Service

The customer service landscape is changing fast in insurance, even without AI. Today, 80% of in-bound calls are often general enquiries or routine transaction requests. Many insurers' call centers are piloting the use of natural language processing to help customers resolve simple, quick-response enquiries such as "when is my next payment?", "when is my policy up for renewal", and "can I change my payment details?" Automating the bulk of in-bound calls will free-up human customer service representatives to focus on complex customer demands and high-touch interactions. As more data is made available to train the processing engine, chatbots will become more sophisticated in service as well as sales, serving ever more needs autonomously as their learning algorithms mature.

In addition to real-time service support, algorithms can be trained to trawl call center voice recordings to identify cross-selling suggestions at time of service. Predictive models will be built based on customer attributes, product portfolios and call center activities to suggest the likelihood of a customer needing and buying a certain product. This will allow customer service representatives to cross-sell while they are servicing the customers on the phone, providing new sources of revenue for the insurers that get this right.

Step 4: Claim

Artificial intelligence will inform claims management in a number of important ways. At a basic level, as with underwriting, machine learning has the potential to automate routine claims processing using machine-learnt judgment to decide whether and how much to pay, and to detect potential fraud.

More sophisticated applications for life and health insurers will have access to near-instant second opinions on medical diagnoses using text-based pattern recognition and AI-driven processing. These technologies already exist and will be deployed by forward-thinking insurers to improve customer guidance, reduce diagnosis error and ensure appropriate treatment for medical conditions.

While many insurers already offer e-claims capabilities to their customers, most medical claims today are still processed manually due to the prevalence of hand-written documentation in the world's healthcare systems. Artificial intelligence will initially take the form of optical character recognition that reads in-patient and outpatient medical information to expedite claims processing. This will be followed by the application of an AI layer on top of the data to perform analysis and gain insights from treatment and claim details. Insights so derived may shine much-needed light on provider behavior, fraud and abuse, excessive charges and consumer behavior, among many others.

Simeon Preston

A world of change

Following a period of wariness of the new and unknown, AI acceptance and adoption will accelerate across all aspects of insurers' customer experience and underlying business operations. With readily accessible AI platform offerings from the likes of Google, Microsoft, Amazon and a thousand start-ups, AI tools are no longer a frontier technology seen as out of reach. AI is increasingly viewed as an achievable path for insurers to pursue, and AI tools will be ever more widely, and progressively, adopted by mainstream companies. An industry historically reliant upon human operators and manual processes is now talking automation and AI. This in turn is causing re-evaluation of why legacy processes persist and how they can be automated or retired, allowing insurance business to be done in altogether more effective, efficient and creative ways.

This building enthusiasm for AI can be seen in the current hype around 'insuretech', a breathless world of ambitious start-ups, corporate accelerators, innovation labs, and ecosystems. Most insurers are seeking to learn, many are building viable prototypes, and some are beginning to deploy AI tools at scale. The emphasis will shift markedly in the next few years from test-and-learn towards large-scale deployment, provided that a few key conditions are satisfied.

Herein lies the challenge for AI in insurance. While the surge in interest and application has generated enthusiasm and opportunity across the industry, AI raises several thorny and as yet unresolved questions in the realms of ethics, employment and regulation.

Take ethics first. All insurance is fundamentally about building and sustaining trust: customers need to be confident that their insurer will treat them fairly over the life of the contract and be there to pay their claim when it comes. For general insurers there is often an annual renewal window, but for life insurers the claim may be decades away. All of the AI tools mentioned in this chapter may, like many other technologies, be put to nefarious as well as beneficent use. At the point of purchase, machine learning algorithms that identify risks a human underwriter might miss – for example, a pattern of personal behavior evident from social media but not declared on an application form – could allow insurers to price risks prohibitively or decline them altogether. At the point of claim, algorithms trained to detect fraud may take a more rigid view of eligibility where expert human adjudicators are able to give benefit of doubt.

From an employment perspective, the portrayal of AI as a large-scale destroyer of jobs is inevitable as the technology advances and adoption grows. AI brings the ability to replicate the human concept of informed decision-making, often with far higher consistency and velocity, which will be especially sensitive in a sector so heavily reliant on repetitive manual processes today. Eventually, most repeated, rules-based tasks requiring an element of judgment will eventually be done automatically and intuitively by AI engines rather than humans. The types of human jobs will adjust and evolve, and many roles – especially those that require a human touch – may actually be enhanced rather than supplanted by the technology. AI may well prove to be empowering for many employees, by creating new kinds of role and new ways of working that we have not yet even imagined.

Moreover, the business changes wrought by AI in insurance will not happen overnight. AI integration will be progressive as corporate confidence grows, and all insurers will have a responsibility to manage the impacts on employees with humanity and respect. Whilst the impacts on some employees will be real and painful, others will be empowered to create new forms of value for customers, organizations and society as a whole.

While corporate ethics and responsibilities will play their part, regulatory uncertainty is perhaps the largest current obstacle to widespread AI adoption in insurance. To ensure fairness and consistency, the industry's regulators require a clear audit trail for decisions taken in underwriting and claims. With AI deployed, this verification may prove hard to provide where the algorithm has made its own judgment at a point in time and adjusted its decision rules since. Moreover, the data and computation requirements of AI often mean its application is most effectively done in the cloud. This is another area of high regulatory uncertainty in an era of tightening rules around outsourcing and data domicile.

With AI technologies evolving so rapidly, regulators themselves will need to keep ahead of AI tool deployments to prevent an uncertain environment in which rules change often, interpretations vary and ambiguities persist. Indeed, regulators may themselves adopt AI-based tools to monitor insurers' actions in more automated ways, so the overall bar is raised for the benefit of all industry participants.

A bright future for the bold

In the coming years, the global insurance industry has the opportunity and ability to transform itself through AI and related technologies. If AI is adopted as widely and as deeply as has been posited above, then the relationships between insurers, customers and regulators will also need to change, both rapidly and soon.

Responsible insurers will ensure that the AI tools they deploy serve to strengthen rather than weaken the bond of trust with their clients: by helping customers learn what protection they need and why; by improving sales effectiveness; by enriching and personalizing service; and by paying claims fairly and fast. Insurers will need to share the financial benefits of large-scale automation and operating efficiencies appropriately between customers, employees and shareholders. They will need to collaborate with regulators on ethical standards, transparency and compliance in a period of large-scale AI adoption and rapid change.

The benefits offered by AI represent a transformational opportunity for those insurers bold enough to seize it. Established competitors' business models, organizations and economics will all face significant adjustment as AI integration raises industry benchmarks for decision-making, customer experience and operating efficiency. At the same time, nimble new entrants will offer AI-based products and services with low unit costs to challenge incumbents' legacy platforms and margins. May the boldest and most responsible AI adopters prevail.

Red Pill – Blue Pill

Marc Lien, Director of Innovation & Digital Development, Lloyds Banking Group

———

In this chapter, Marc shares his perspectives of transforming Lloyds Banking Group – the UK's largest retail and commercial bank – towards a data and analytics-driven enterprise to be the best bank for customers and to help Britain prosper.

"This is your last chance. After this there is no turning back. You take the blue pill: the story ends, you wake up in your bed and believe whatever you want to believe. You take the red pill: you stay in Wonderland and I show you how deep the rabbit-hole goes." - Morpheus, *The Matrix* (1999)[i]

In almost every data discovery project there comes a red-pill-blue-pill moment. In *The Matrix*, the main character Neo is offered the choice between two pills. The blue pill would lead him to stay in the Matrix, maintaining the status quo and blissful ignorance of the world. The red pill would involve experiencing a new truth about how the world really works, one that is unfamiliar and could be harsh and difficult for him.

Most projects that work to apply data science to new business domains commence with teams doing initial value discovery work to identify quick wins and incremental improvements. These are like manna from heaven for the business executive. Quick wins allow them to address some of the perennial pain points their team have been suffering from (e.g. lack of data, data quality, model cycle time). Incremental changes show line of sight to 10-20% improvements in both business efficiency and effectiveness.

In the same discovery exercise, teams invariably come up with an alternative future, one that is equivalent to the leap-of-faith of the red pill. This reimagines the same business but from scratch, with an intelligent and learning algorithm as its core. A complete pivot from smart people making periodic judgements on scarce insight, to intelligent machines looking at all the data in real-time and guiding the smart people on where to spend their energy. These machines both automate and augment. The promise is business performance that is two to ten times of that today.

As the MD of the business, do you take the blue pill – quick wins to assuage the team and line of sight on familiar ground to deliver your budget? Or do you take the red pill – a complete reimagining of the business using less familiar methods, organization upheaval but the (untested) promise of delivering superhero performance improvements of two to ten times?

It takes a brave MD to take the leap.

However amazing your data science team is, whatever brilliant algorithmic future they envisage, the ability to have an impact is entirely dependent on persuading MDs around the business to make this choice. Without this, the data science team's promise of great things will be a chasm versus a reality of next to no change. Bringing Applied Data Science to enterprise scale is predominantly a people change management challenge, with a little bit of data science and a little bit of data engineering. Not the other way around.

Luckily, we can choose both routes, take both pills, and deliver a portfolio of interventions. Firstly, quick wins which bring the team along and deliver incremental impact. They also happen to be the foundations to enable a more transformative system. Second, build a challenger model – an enterprise start-up if you like – which the business runs in parallel for six months measuring and comparing performance. This builds confidence in the new algorithmic methods and shapes an environment where there is permission to do things differently. After six months, either incremental improvement is good enough and you can shut down the start-up, or the challenger performance is so much improved – and evidenced as such – that investing further to scale the start-up and roll-in BAU activities is less of a risk.

You need to run several of these enterprise start-ups in parallel. The world outside your organization is moving too quickly to allow for toe-dipping sequencing of initiatives. If you want to transform your organization, you need to focus on scaling and go beyond experimental labs. Test and learn at small scale and low cost.

At Lloyds Banking Group, we are transforming the customer experience and our business in order to be the best bank for customers and help Britain prosper. Our transformation investments and activities have data science and advanced analytics at their core, working through a portfolio of these enterprise start-ups. Here are three examples:

Customer experience

Digital interfaces to banking services are rapidly evolving. The advent of cognitive services – chatbots or virtual service agents – encourage deeper engagement than a standard banking app through the more accessible conversational interfaces. The bots can simultaneously reduce the cost of customer service, whilst providing customers with new forms of value – contextual insights and recommendations, reaching a customer base increasingly living on messaging apps. At Lloyds Banking Group, we have been experimenting with where virtual assistants can provide 24/7 support to customers who get stuck in the self-service digital journeys and end up phoning customer services. Virtual agents present customers with the option of having a conversation to resolve their issue or to be passed on to a human. In the domains where we have trained the robot, we have seen very promising results. Not only is the bot able to resolve a high proportion of customer queries but customers are on the whole supportive. The enterprise start-up focused initially on one specific use case. Based on the transformational impact, we are in the midst of scaling, led by what our customers are telling us.

Risk management

Protecting our customers is of utmost importance. We've augmented our roadmap of cyber and fraud investments with an enterprise start-up that has applied a host of machine learning, deep learning and advanced graphing methods to provide better identification of transaction fraud, reduce falsely flagged transactions, introduce new predictive algorithms, and analyze fraud patterns and anomalies.

Productivity enhancement

How do you decide where's best to focus the efforts of one of the most scarce and valuable resources we have – the experts? By developing intelligent machines that can analyze large swaths of data, we've been able to rely on these algorithms to propose what the experts prioritize and where they spend their time. This has been applicable across businesses and functional areas. Agent Smith in *The Matrix* says *"Never send a human to do a machine's job."*[ii] AI and machine learning may very well be part of the solution to the productivity quandary we've been puzzled by in service-driven Western economies for the last decade. We've found that new techniques such as natural language generation and natural language processing are particularly exciting avenues for development and application.

So where do you start? As Morpheus says: *"Neo, sooner or later you're going to realize just as I did that there's a difference between knowing the path and walking the path."* [iii]

Start by starting.

---

[i]   *The Matrix*, Silver Pictures (1999)
[ii]   *The Matrix*
[iii] *The Matrix*

How Could Natural Language Dialogue Change the Future of Life and Business?

Michael Wei, Director of AI Research Center, Samsung

Michael Wei is Director of Samsung AI research in US. In this position, he is responsible for technology strategy, research roadmaps and key projects. Prior to Samsung, Michael was Director of Huawei's AI lab. He has 15 years' expertise in intelligence technology, holding various positions at Lucent Bell Labs, IBM Watson and A.T. Kearney. Michael received his MBA from The University of Texas at Austin and master's in Computer Science from the University of Southern California.

The dream of a 'talking machine'

In his famous paper, "Computing Machinery and Intelligence", written in 1950, Turing introduced a test of a machine's intelligent capability by conducting natural language conversation with humans. Since then, the dream of a 'talking machine' that can assist, entertain, and communicate with humans has never stopped.

'Talking machine' is of interest to not only scientists but also business leaders. In Steve Jobs's last several months in Apple, he still dedicated himself to the acquisition of Siri because he shrewdly envisioned the voice interface to be the key component for the next generation of personal devices. History has repeatedly demonstrated that the human machine interface (HMI) is the primary driving force for the paradigm shift of the computing platform. The multiple-touchscreen enabled one-hand operation, so convenient that it made the internet available anytime and anywhere, fully utilizing the user's fragmented time. It created such an addictive experience that permanently changed the users' behavior and social interaction. Comparatively, in the mid-1990s, when the web browser and Windows 95 led the surge of the internet, the small rolling tool (mouse) played such a critical role that the primary business model of even today's internet is measured by 'click-through'. It all makes sense as "what technology wants is what human wants"[i] – the most successful innovation is the one that alters humans' behavior permanently and HMI technology is the right medium to accomplish that.

Surge of personal assistant and early success

By December 2016, Amazon Echo had recorded 5.1m shipments since its debut in late 2014. Google Home has booked between 400,000 to 500,000 sales since its launch in late 2016. The voice interface device has led an exponential growth, a phenomenon comparable to the paradigm of the smartphone. According to a recent survey released by VoiceLabs in January 2017, the combined shipment of

Amazon Echo and Google Home in 2017 is estimated to be 24.5m, more than a 300% increase over last year.[ii]

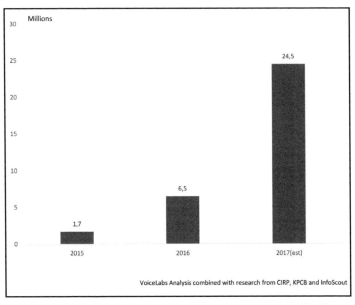

Figure 1: Annual Shipment of Voice Interface Devices (Credit: Michael Wei[iii])

The primary drive behind the surge of voice interface is the historical breakthrough of ASR (Automated Speech Recognition) technology. Ever since deep learning was applied to ASR in 2009, the accuracy has jumped from nearly 70% to about 95%, which is considered to be close to human level capability.[iv] With the help of hardware like Microphone Array, the state-of-the-art technology also functions well in noisy and far-reaching circumstances, as Amazon Echo has proved.

Consumers are fond of the voice interface because it is not only fun but also convenient to use. Voice breaks the physical constraints of device interaction and enables scenarios that were previously not well-served by physical-contact-based HMI (Human Machine Interaction) technologies such as touchscreen, keyboard and mouse. According to a KPCP report in June 2016, more than 20% of internet searches are already done via the voice interface.[v]

Despite the rapid growth of voice interface, we are still at the very early stage of this 'talking machine' dream. Most current consumers are sticking to off-the-shelf actions like streaming music, reading audiobooks, seeking simple information and controlling smart devices. The technology is not yet sufficiently matured to support sophisticated and flexible conversation. However, in the coming years, we will see increasing numbers of devices as well as applications on this new platform. The most exciting and impactful technologies will be natural language conversation engines that enable deeper and richer interactions between machine and human.

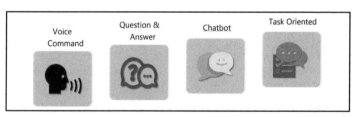

Figure 2: Four Types of Conversational AI
(Credit: Michael Wei, Samsung Research America)

Four types of conversational AI

Natural language dialogue spreads across a wide range, and it is important to understand the difference. Generally speaking, there are four types, each with a specific goal and distinct supporting technology behind them.

(1) The first type of dialogue system is **Voice Command**, largely enabled by automated speech recognition (ASR) and a rule-based engine. Amazon Echo started with this type.

(2) The second that came to the market is **Question Answering**, of which the core technology is Knowledge Graph and search engine. IBM's Watson and Siri are early examples of this type.

(3) The third one is **Chatbot**, with capability of flexible conversation. Google researchers Oriol Vinyals and Quoc Le built a deep learning system that showed potential to carry forward meaningful human level conversation.[vi]

(4) The last and also the most technologically difficult one is **Task-Oriented Dialogue**, which differs from "Chatbot" by its capability to maintain purposefulness during the long process of conversation, in order to accomplish specific tasks or goals.

The four types of conversational AI have different maturity in terms of technology and market. Voice command and question answering are already in the market. Chatbots, especially for education and companion purpose, are on the horizon. Task-oriented dialogue is the new frontier that will enable a huge number of business opportunities. Most technologies of the last type are still in the lab, but will likely to appear in the market in the next five years.

Three waves moving forward

Market penetration of new technology is difficult for it has to solve either the different problems that existing technology cannot touch, or the same problem ten times better for consumers to make the switch. Luckily, for the innovators from all over the world, there are so many areas in conversational AI for them to reinvent the future of life and business. The market penetration is likely to happen in three waves.

The first wave will be the 'no hand, no eye' market that are blind spots for mobile devices. Amazon Echo has shown us a perfect and successful example of creating a new market by using this advanced technology. The increased number of micro-interactions at home serves as a perfect market for a dialogue system because voice is beyond physical reach and convenience to use. Another 'no hand, no eye' scenario will be in automotive, especially with the rise of driverless cars.

The nuance is that the automotive industry normally has longer development cycles of often two to three years. Therefore, this market will be an early adopter, but probably won't be among the first ones to appear in the market.

The second wave will be call center and technical support. New technology, especially the one with cost-saving potential, is always appealing to business, as the ROI is relatively easier to calculate, therefore more convincing in business environments. However, for this specific market, there are still user experience hurdles to overcome. Automated customer service has already been used in call centers for over 10 years. Till today, the technologies are mostly scripted and limited, due to the insufficiency of technology to generate satisfactory user experiences in a complex space. With the latest deep learning, we are currently at the edge of opening a much bigger portion of this market in the next three years.

The third wave will be in the so-called 'exploratory services' in ecommerce, medical, legal and financial, etc. It will widely democratize the knowledge of specific domains and make it much more widely accessible; hence, it will deeply impact everyone's life and enable a brand-new era of internet: 'on-demand knowledge'. This is also the ultimate goal of natural language scientists. However, the current technology still has a steep curve to overcome and may need several significant breakthroughs in the coming years for it to happen. A truly flexible and purposeful dialogue system might still be more than five years out.

The future

Every generation has its own products that it is naturally born with. In my generation, our first experience with the computer was PC, laptop, mouse and keyboard. My five-year-old daughter was born with touchscreens – finger-clicking and swiping is naturally intuitive to her interaction with machines. For the kids who will be born in the next couple of years, an environment with talking machines will be just part of their lives.

First of all, it upholds the era of 'Chatware'. Voice interface has the potential to be the new converged interface for future internet users. The Google search bar will no longer be the default place for information. Upon looking for information, people can simply ask the machine. The shift of the internet is continuous. For the generation who were born with social media, they are more likely to go to their friends if questions arise, instead of Googling it. It generates substantial value to consumers as it solves the big challenge of mobile – too many applications. Instead of having hundreds of thousands of apps, there could be a few universal interfaces empowered by natural-dialogue technology, behind which is a variety of services and information sources. For companies, instead of developing front-end apps, they only need to develop the back-end service which receives API calls from a voice interface.

Secondly, it empowers a much more adaptive and personalized service. Voice is very personal, much more so than existing HMI methods. Personal identity and contextual information can be gauged from the conversation, and be leveraged for a more personalized service. Better still, voice carries sentiment information which will provide more feedback for the system for further improvement. It has the potential to create a sentimental bond between device and people.

Thirdly, democratization of domain knowledge. Several industries are established by exclusive access to domain knowledge. Technical support and sales for one instance, health, legal and financial consulting for another. A lot of problems in those domains is not as simple as finding the answer to a specific question, but rather how to explore through the problem space to better define the question in order to find the answer to it. Conversation AI technologies can certainly help automate this exploratory process, starting with areas with relatively small problem space, and gradually moving into much more complex use cases.

Lastly, it calls for more innovations on security. Unlike physical contact, voice is weak on security solutions, which creates a large space for innovators. Consumers certainly don't want an unauthorized user to make the purchase or find out information that they should not. Parents would likely insist to restrict several internet information services from being accessible to their kids, or any kids. All this will require stronger security methods integrated with the future products.

Being the most natural communication method for humans, natural language has the potential to permanently change the way we interact with machines and the internet. Just as touchscreen helped realize the phenomena of mobile internet, dialogue will be the enabling technology for the next era of internet by serving as the universal interface to information and services.

[i]   'What Technology Wants', Kevin Kelly, (London: Penguin Books, 2011)

[ii]   http://voicelabs.co/2017/01/15/the-2017-voice-report/

[iii]   Data taken from: http://voicelabs.co/2017/01/15/the-2017-voice-report/

[iv]   https://blogs.microsoft.com/next/2016/10/18/historic-achievement-microsoft-researchers-reach-human-parity-conversational-speech-recognition/

[v]   http://www.kpcb.com/internet-trends

[vi]   https://www.wired.com/2015/06/google-made-chatbot-debates-meaning-life/

Cyber Security in the Age of Automation

Nicole Eagan, CEO, Darktrace

As Chief Executive Officer of Darktrace, Nicole Eagan has positioned the company as an international leader in cyber defense. Nicole was named 'Woman of the Year' at the 2016 Cyber Security Awards for successfully introducing disruptive machine learning technology to the global market. Her extensive career as a technology executive includes over 25 years of commercial and marketing experience. An expert in developing and executing strategies for high-growth businesses, Nicole helped Darktrace secure $65 million in Series C funding from KKR and led the company to 600% year-on-year growth. Under her leadership, Darktrace's innovative approach to cyber security has won over 20 awards, including World Economic Forum Technology Pioneer. The company is headquartered in San Francisco, CA and Cambridge, England and now has more than 360 employees working across 23 countries.

Recent advances in machine learning (ML) and artificial intelligence (AI) have equipped us to handle an unprecedented level of complexity, and modern businesses have embraced these innovations wholeheartedly. Complicated tasks that used to take specialists hours to complete can now be done by a machine, automatically and instantaneously.

Companies like Google and Amazon use advanced algorithms to intelligently rank search results. Self-driving cars are powered by ML. Indoor farms harness AI to adjust lighting and temperature. And natural disasters like earthquakes can now be predicted using automated technology. Advancements like these have ushered in a new era: the 'Age of Automation'.

But for cyber security, automation hasn't just empowered defenders. It's also emboldened the attackers. In years gone by, the threat landscape was dominated by phishing scams and basic computer viruses. Today's most advanced threats, by contrast, represent a new class of malware. They can operate without human oversight, and they're capable of perpetuating and propagating from within the network. By 2020, or even sooner, these AI-powered cyber-attacks will become the new norm.

Sophisticated attacks like these are consistently overwhelming modern security tools. But to understand how this situation came to be, and to understand the future of cyber-warfare, first we have to go back to the beginning – to a time before autonomous attackers and defenders were locked in an ongoing cyber battle. In the beginning, there was peace.

The dawn of cyber security

It all started in 1969 with an internet precursor called ARPANET[i]. The Pentagon-backed project aimed to create an interconnected network of individual machines, which would eventually evolve into the modern-day internet.

ARPANET was an interesting experiment, but it never occurred to anyone that a network of a few thousand computers would one day be used for massive, billion-dollar hacks. Think of ARPANET as ground zero for cyber security. There was nothing to protect, and no attacks to prevent. This 'peace' lasted for nearly two decades. But in 1988, a graduate student named Robert Morris changed everything.

As part of his research project at Cornell, Morris set out to measure the size of the internet, which by the late 1980s had expanded well beyond the confines of ARPANET[ii]. His idea was to exploit vulnerabilities in Unix systems to determine the number of existing connections. However, Morris made a critical mistake. A small programming error caused his program to infect machines repeatedly, instead of just once. The resulting deluge of network traffic quickly overwhelmed the network and shut down large swaths of the internet. The attack became known as a 'worm' and it was the first cyber-attack in history.

According to most estimates, the worm infected a mere 6,000 computers, which is a miniscule number by modern standards. By comparison, the Yahoo breach of 2013 compromised over 1 billion users[iii]. But Morris' mistake demonstrated a fundamental flaw in network architecture, and future attacks were sure to come. The incident prompted DARPA (Defense Advanced Research Projects Agency) to create a coordinate response system to mitigate network downtime. Just like that, the cyber security industry was born.

But ever since then, cyber security has been playing catch-up. The process quickly proved to be cyclical: an attacker found a vulnerability, and a defender developed a solution; always in that order. In other words, the defenders never knew what to defend against until after the attack occurred. This was true with Morris' worm and, for the most part, it's still true today.

By the time defenders learned how to prevent another worm attack, there was already a new kind of threat to deal with. Once again, cyber security was forced into reactive mode. Computer viruses spawned anti-virus software, phishing attacks led to anti-spam software, and so on. Each new wave of attacks prompted a new security measure, and cyber security became an industry of patchwork defences, plugging holes as fast as they appeared.

I'd like to say we're at a unique point in time where we finally *do* know where technology — and therefore cyber-attacks — will go next. But that would miss the point. The truth is, we don't know. We've never known. That's why the attackers have always been one step ahead. The solution, then, has to incorporate adaptive, evolving, and intelligent technology that can defend against the entire spectrum of threat, both known and unknown. In this way, we can embrace the uncertainty that has always defined the industry.

Machine-versus-machine warfare

Nowhere is this uncertainty more prevalent than in the realm of artificial intelligence. As cyber-attacks start to become powered by AI, they'll become impossible to predict, and worse, they'll be effectively invisible to legacy security tools. These tools can only block threats that match the signature of known attacks. AI attacks, on the other hand, represent a different category of threat altogether — the 'unknown unknown'.

In many ways, the 'unknown unknown' attack is like an outbreak of a disease we couldn't predict. Without knowing anything about the disease, we would have no vaccines to inoculate ourselves with. However, where traditional methods fail, our immune system picks up the slack. Even though our immune system doesn't recognize the disease, it can recognize that it's not a part of us, and is therefore dangerous. In that way, our immune system can neutralize even the most serious threats without knowing what to look for.

To protect against AI attacks, cyber security should operate on the same principle. Such a security system would use AI algorithms to learn what is and what is not normal network behavior. Without relying on knowledge of past attacks, it could defend against all types of threats — including those we didn't know existed. Then, the same way our immune system responds with antibodies, this approach would fight cyber-threats with automated, proportionate responses.

Machine-versus-machine warfare like this is not some distant fiction. At Darktrace, our technology has given us a rare glimpse into the ways that modern criminals are using automation. The first thing that's become apparent to us is that the 'Age of Automation' hasn't just benefited the good guys. As we continue to automate our defenses, criminals have twisted modern innovations to breed fully autonomous cyber-attacks.

More and more, threats are starting to move at machine-speeds and carry out their missions without a human operator. For example, a European telecommunications firm was recently infected with an aggressive strain of ransomware – a type of malware that encrypts files and holds them hostage. In a matter of seconds, the infected device contacted the Dark Web and started to automatically encrypt company documents.

Another attack – this time against a healthcare organization – repeatedly copied itself and automatically infected every device it touched. The more the malware copied itself, the deeper it burrowed into the network as it searched for valuable data.

Self-replicating attacks have been around for years. And yet, these were different. By leveraging modern innovations, traditional attacks have been supercharged with automated technology. Attacks like these have started to exhibit signs of what can only be called intelligence.

Silent, stealthy, and intelligent

Consider the age-old phishing attack. By now, you can probably spot a Nigerian Prince scam from a mile away. But the phishing attacks of the future will be different. By using AI to learn a person's unique writing style, machines will be able to autonomously craft convincing emails. For instance, say a message from your boss appears in your inbox. It sounds like her. It uses her email signature. It's even from her actual address, and she's asking you to review an attached PDF. Would you open it?

And as voice recognition technology like Amazon's Alexa and Microsoft's Cortana have gone mainstream, attackers will start to co-opt it for nefarious ends. Imagine getting a phone call from a potential landlord asking for your Social Security number. He stresses that it's vital for your rental application. Except on the other line, it's only a robot that sounds remarkably like him. Would you respond?

These are the attacks of the future, and they won't just target individuals. Artificial intelligence will take aim at dismantling entire businesses through subtle, insidious methods. By iteratively adapting themselves to evade internal security, AI attacks will be able to blend in seamlessly with the noise of a busy corporate network. A threat could sit quietly for years, gathering intelligence and learning the network. Then, once a month, it could activate for a few milliseconds and manipulate sensitive data.

For example, it could change data from an oilfield sensor that a gas company uses to buy mining rights. By tricking them into drilling in a depleted area, the company would take massive losses, and nobody would know why. Similarly, an AI attack could alter the mathematical models that inform boardroom decisions at a Wall Street company, thus forcing them to make bad investments. In this way, AI attacks will arm criminals and competing businesses alike with the means to engage in corporate sabotage on a previously unimaginable scale, with millions of dollars at stake.

Digital assets won't be the only target for AI attacks. They'll also be able to take control of critical business equipment. An AI attack could exploit vulnerabilities in the Internet of Things to sabotage manufacturing equipment, quality control machines, infrastructure like subways and trains, or even healthcare equipment like MRIs or pacemakers. By holding these machines hostage, organizations would be at the mercy of an automated, malicious machine.

The key theme here is that AI attacks, by definition, will be impossible to predict. They'll be able to manifest themselves in any number of forms, target a range of critical business assets, and dynamically evolve to avoid traditional security systems. If we resort to defending against a specific type of AI attack, we've already lost. Defending against these attacks will involve much more than erecting pre-emptive barriers.

Machine learning and the future of cyber defense

Today's most cutting-edge security systems don't make any assumptions about how, when, or where an attack will strike. Through the power of unsupervised machine learning, they can detect cyber-threats without reference to past attacks. The technology can intelligently find patterns and draw conclusions without being programmed to find only *specific* patterns or draw only *certain* conclusions.

By capturing raw network traffic – which can contain millions of constantly changing data points – unsupervised machine learning can be used to understand that data on a deep level. Without a human controller, the technology uses that data to build a picture of normal network behavior and spot deviations that indicate potential threats.

From there, AI defenses can automatically fight back by isolating, slowing down, and neutralizing in-progress threats. In this way, they can mimic the self-learning mechanisms of the human immune system to fight back against the entire range of cyber-attacks – including those powered by AI.

This is the future of AI in business: machines fighting machines in a battle for network dominance. AI attacks will be too fast-moving, too complex, and too evasive for traditional tools or human security teams to handle. That's why AI and automation will be essential in the fight for network control.

By harnessing the power of unsupervised machine learning, organizations will be able to protect their assets from modern, automated attacks as well as the sophisticated AI attacks of the near-future. In this way, organizations can get ahead of the threat for the first time in history.

[i]   Defense Advanced Research Projects Agency, *ARPANET and the Origins of the Internet*, http://www.darpa.mil/about-us/timeline/arpanet.

[ii]   Timothy Lee, "How a grad student trying to build the first botnet brought the Internet to its knees," *The Washington Post*, Nov. 1, 2013

[iii] Sam Thielman, "Yahoo hack: 1bn accounts compromised by biggest data breach in history," *The Guardian*, Dec. 15, 2016

Autonomics and a Pro-Human Way

Kalyan Kumar, CTO, HCL Technologies

Kalyan Kumar B. (KK) is the Global CTO of HCL Technologies. KK leads 'Global Product and Technology Organization' and is the leader of DRYiCE Business Unit, a unified autonomics and orchestration platform business, which HCL have positioned as the core foundation of the 21st century enterprise. Additionally, he oversees the cloud services business unit across all service lines within HCL.

In his current role, KK is responsible for defining product and technology strategies, developing new offerings and solutions, and managing practice and service-line lifecycles across 'next generation IT and operations', 'cloud and autonomics/service orchestration, and 'leveraged platform-centric delivery for DRYiCE', and 'leveraged cloud services'.

An exciting new partnership is emerging between humans and machines. Unlike any interaction witnessed in history, this powerful teamwork promises unprecedented benefits to business, people and the economy. We are already cognizant of the immense power of automation in driving efficiency, productivity, agility, adaptability and optimization across industries. The fact is that automation is no longer an option in today's 21st century enterprise. Yet, there has been growing apprehension about its impact on jobs – among other things.

Like many who have witnessed first-hand the tremendous technological progress over the past two decades, I believe the fear is misinformed. In fact, I am convinced that automation – or its evolved avatar 'autonomics', which includes the application of modern-day miracles such as artificial intelligence (AI), robotics, cognitive computing, machine learning and analytics – is perhaps the greatest opportunity the world has been presented with in a long time. Moving the impact of autonomics further into the 'orchestration zone' enables businesses to become sentient and react quickly to changing market conditions. Together, autonomics and orchestration represent an opportunity to meet the myriad escalating challenges of the 21st century head-on, with the full intellectual and technological might of the human race.

As is true for any revolutionary concept or endeavor – the true potential of autonomics can only be realized with considered and methodical proliferation. Spearheading IT transformation projects for more than a decade, I have realized that any transformation, including automation, is a journey that is first-and-foremost steeped in pragmatism. It is easy to get excited with cool technology advancements, but what good are those if not aligned to desired business and human outcomes? Pivoting to an IT perspective, application of automation requires a deep assessment of prevailing organizational structures and IT landscapes, their inter-dependencies and affected ecosystems, before applying autonomics technologies in a phased manner – all while keeping humans at the center.

There is only one way to make automation work right and that is the pro-human way. Done right, automation is a perfect showcase of the collaboration between humans and technology that opens up vast unseen opportunities.

Think of the word 'automation'. What do you visualize? Humanoids in our offices? Robots running our factories? Driverless cars on the roads? Watson, Deep Blue, AlphaGo? I have often been asked about my views on this fascinating subject as an insider in this world.

As I see it, automation is far from an 'edge-of-the-seat sci-fi thriller' that you might imagine; it is rather a subtle but hard-nosed business-driven technology strategy that can make organizations more efficient and individuals more productive when evolved into its more potent avatar, autonomics. The evolution of automation to autonomics is much more than an incremental change; it is a transformation that is being driven by innovative application of modern-day miracles such as AI, robotics, cognitive computing, machine learning, Big Data analytics, and many others.

The technologies behind this evolution have been around for some time now, so it should not come as a surprise to anyone whose profession is centered on technology. But the sheer velocity at which this evolution has happened is what has left many organizations unprepared to deal with its consequences; resulting in misinformed apprehension.

Let's dig deeper into this brave new world of autonomics.

Traditional automation has been around for at least a decade. I have fond memories of the rush we felt when we developed solutions for our customers with technologies like scripts-based automation enabled by cool (at the time!) IT systems management tools. Enterprises have always had this inexorable drive to reduce cost and eliminate waste, and these IT task-based automation technologies are now ubiquitous in any modern IT landscape.

Then the cloud happened.

While tomes have been written – and are still being written – on the impact of cloud computing on enterprises, I believe that, primarily, cloud technologies set the world on an irreversible path toward becoming software-defined. The result of having almost every component in a traditional IT architecture – databases, servers, applications, services – accessible through web APIs provided impetus to the evolution of traditional automation technologies into something far more intelligent and autonomous. Easy over-the-web accessibility opened the doors to cross-pollination from adjacent technology advancements – especially pattern recognition, AI, machine learning, and predictive analytics. The impact has been quick and sweeping, with the airwaves erupting with news and views about how AI-related technologies can transform enterprise IT. What's so amazing about autonomics? Let me explain.

While traditional automation still relied on humans doing the grunt-work – sorting through the noise and making decisions, hence exposing the enterprise to human errors and delays – the application of AI-related technologies promises a way round that. Now IT systems, through the power of autonomics, not only automate the task, but automate a lot of the hard, thankless work of sorting through events, logs, service requests, etc. – and suggest the best probable courses of action to IT admins. Not only that, autonomics systems can – after adequate training – recognize typical event or error patterns, take automated decisions and trigger appropriate actions through scripts. Let us try to understand the real impact of this.

Does autonomics eliminate the need for an IT admin? No, it doesn't, as only in a perfect world do all errors and events follow predefined patterns. Does autonomics reduce the load on IT admins and enable them to make smarter decisions? Yes, as it eliminates noise and provides 'curated' information to the IT staff. Does autonomics result in overall simplification of managing and ensuring IT systems' availability and performance levels? Absolutely!

Just think about it. If autonomics allows typically stressed and over-worked IT staff to save time and focus on higher-level issues, eliminates unnecessary noise and confusion and automates execution of common IT tasks, the end result is much more than just 'efficiency'. It is simplicity.

Imagine a scenario where the best of external and internal services can be easily procured and integrated to create seamless and differentiating experiences for end-users. Imagine if business could 'orchestrate' unique experiences across multiple dimensions at the push of a button. That is what the combined power of autonomics and orchestration does. It creates a scenario where IT can drive business outcomes by keeping complexity and costs in check; procuring and integrating apps, services and micro-services from internal and external sources; enabling multi-vendor process harmony by aligning individual SLAs into Business SLAs; providing true business agility and outcome-orientation; and synchronizing all the touchpoints to help achieve business outcomes by rapidly crafting a truly unified experience for end users.

How a Fortune 500 manufacturing company began their journey to lean and agile with automation

Usually, the first step to transformation is to admit that something is wrong. One of HCL's oldest customers, and a leading global brand in the manufacturing industry, recently found themselves at a crossroad. This story begins when (after some soul-searching) they realized that to continue delivering on their brand's promise and stay competitive in a shifting market, they had to renew focus on customer and employee experience. While a larger business strategy was in place, they realized that technology was a key component of their plan; and was also turning out to be, in large part, what was holding them back. The problems started in the foundation, where IT managers supporting business initiatives with applications and websites took up to 60 days to provision something as critical (and basic) as a physical server. Furthermore, the whole process of provisioning IT resources was manual and was prone to errors, leading to a substandard experience for IT employees and their stakeholders. Lack of any kind of remote management functionality resulted in far less than optimal usage of their five data centers, which ended up operating in monolithic silos. These were not uncommon issues, but our customer decided to do something about them.

They quickly realized, with the help of some sound advice, that automation was necessary to bring the overall level of experience up. But before that, the need was to increase virtualization levels and reduce dependence on physical servers. While that was being done, they partnered with HCL to implement MyCloud®, a proven automated cloud management platform and core component of HCL's

DryICE® autonomics platform. MyCloud enabled a sleek, catalog-based interface which significantly improved the process and the experience for IT and for their stakeholders. While this had direct impact on productivity and satisfaction, what really gave business a shot in the arm was the use of automation to bring down server provisioning time from 30 days to four hours. Did this lead to a reduction in IT staff? Not at all. This led to a happier staff which could focus on supporting rapid business growth at the pace that was needed. This transformation led to a better relationship between IT and their stakeholders.

So, in the case of our customer, was automation technology the sole hero? Far from it. It required a whole slew of associated changes at the infrastructure level, firm policies which discouraged use of physical servers and incentivized usage of virtualization. It required close human collaboration between the company and HCL. It required focused change management and effective communication to all involved stakeholders. But most of all it required investment and commitment from the leadership who believed in the long-term benefits of automation-led transformation enough to fight the *status quo*.

How one of America's most prominent not-for-profit organizations used operations automation to effectively deliver millions of smiles

This is one of my favorite stories. One that I am especially proud of, because of the direct impact we helped create on millions of lives. Our esteemed customer has been serving their target demographic with life-changing services since the 1950s. Over the past few years, HCL has been helping them keep up with the times through the power of IT. But as is common in these times of massive change in customer expectations, they were coerced into raising their already high standards of customer experience on their websites, web applications and mobile applications. Being a not-for-profit, they were not driven by market pressures as much as by a genuine intent to improve the overall experience of their customers. Being a not-for-profit, they also had to be prudent about maintaining current team levels, while endeavoring to deliver a much better experience. Automation seemed to be the only way out of this gridlock.

Enterprise architects and change agents from both sides of the table evaluated the various options and, after a thorough cost-benefit analysis, came up with a solution based on ElasticOps – a platform operations automation service delivered on the back of DryICE®. ElasticOps, as the name suggests, allows IT operations supporting web, mobile and digital platforms to scale up and down intelligently and on demand. ElasticOps, using the power of AI and machine learning, was able to learn from historical load patterns, and dynamically manage platform performance by scaling infrastructure up or down. Not only that, it provided intelligent analytics on operations, upcoming changes in traffic patterns, spikes in bandwidth requirements and other important operational information to IT and business users, allowing them to make intelligent decisions before critical incidents occurred.

The end result? Our customer today is able to leverage the real power of AI and impact the lives of millions of their customers in a positive way by eliminating application slowdowns and downtimes – no matter what time of year or what the traffic load. All this while maintaining current IT staffing levels. If this is not the pro-human impact of AI, what is?

The undeniable fact is that we are in a period of unprecedented change sparked by technology. We are entering a new and very different phase where automation – or autonomics as we call it, including AI, robotics, machine learning and analytics – will change the workplace as we know it. But this is certainly not the first time we are undergoing transition. Call it Joseph Schumpeter's "creative destruction"[i] or John Maynard Keynes' "technological unemployment",[ii] we have been through stormy periods of adjustment before. And, without a doubt, we will do so again.

As Microsoft CEO Satya Nadella wrote recently, "The beauty of machines and humans working in tandem gets lost in the discussion about whether AI is a good thing or a bad thing."[iii] I could not agree more. I truly believe that autonomics is the greatest opportunity presented to business worldwide in a long time. An opportunity in which we can rediscover the lost key to economic progress through the power of technology. But to do so, we have to overcome our fears and surf the crest of the wave to make it net positive by recognizing three basic principles. To make it simple, let me call them the three Ps: Partnership, Process and Planning.

Partnership

Historically, each major technological development emerges from a collaboration between people and technology. A scenario that has always been by the people and for the people. An automation-enabled tomorrow would too follow the same ground rule. Yes, the power of AI is spectacular. But it pales in comparison to the power of 'augmented intelligence' – a partnership between humans and machines.

Process

This turns the spotlight on the basic premise of automation. The fact that it automates activities and not jobs. Therefore, the focus needs to shift from reduction in jobs to redefinition of processes. An in-depth study into workplace automation by McKinsey drew a similar core insight, concluding: "The road ahead is less about automating individual jobs wholesale, than it is about automating the activities within occupations and redefining roles and processes."[iv] And, the possibility to automate certain activities opens up vast opportunities for augmentation of roles played by people in the workplace.

Planning

This is the part that is completely controlled by people. As leading technologists and economists have pointed out, the idea of robots taking away jobs is based on the assumption that "we are powerless to alter or shape the effects of technological change on labor". To be successful and sustainable, autonomics is and must be a pragmatic pro-human journey. One that is undertaken in waves, based on the maturity of the prevalent IT within an organization.

Most importantly, it must be accompanied by a successful up-placement of the workforce at every stage – a fact that, apparently, is already recognized by several businesses. Studying the impact of industrial robots on manufacturing in 17 developed countries, the London School of Economics found that while robots did seem to replace some jobs, their most important impact was to significantly increase the productivity of the factories, creating new jobs for other workers.[v]

There is no turning away from the fact that technology has been a lifeline of human progress. The hype and fear we are seeing around us undermines not just the power of technology, but also the power of the human mind. As we enter uncharted territories, we need to keep the faith in a collaborative way forward fueled by a human-machine partnership rather than look for roadmaps of assurance. And I am not alone in this belief. Berkeley roboticist Ken Goldberg proposes replacing the 'singularity' approach with 'multiplicity', with diverse groups of humans and machines solving problems through collaboration.[vi] Stanford roboticist Sebastian Thrun, who started the Google self-driving-car project, is driven by the belief that "technology progresses by complementing people rather than replacing them".[vii] And Nadella points out that, guided by the right values, principles and skills, this initial phase of invention will be followed by subsequent phases when we "retrofit for the future" and navigate the "distortion, dissonance and dislocation" to ultimately progress as humans and as a society.[viii] I believe automation is a new frontier of this human-machine partnership; one that will be good for business, good for people and great for society as a whole.

Kalyan Kumar

i   Joseph Schumpeter, *Capitalism, Socialism and Democracy* (New York: Harper, 1975) [orig. pub. 1942], pp. 82-85:

ii   John Maynard Keynes, 'Economic Possibilities for our Grandchildren' (1930): http://www.econ.yale.edu/smith/econ116a/keynes1.pdf

iii   http://www.information-age.com/robots-wont-replace-humans-123464364/

iv   http://www.mckinsey.com/business-functions/digital-mckinsey/our-insights/four-fundamentals-of-workplace-automation

v   http://cep.lse.ac.uk/pubs/download/dp1335.pdf

vi   https://www.nytimes.com/2015/05/26/science/darpa-robotics-challenge-terminator.html?_r=0

vii https://www.nytimes.com/2015/05/26/science/darpa-robotics-challenge-terminator.html?_r=0

viii http://www.information-age.com/robots-wont-replace-humans-123464364/

144

The Beginning of a New Era

Robert Woolliams, Head of Research, AI Business

_____

Robert Woolliams heads AI Business research-related projects, including publishing projects, industry reports, and solution provider research and interviews, while also assisting the Content Director with AI Summit speaker management. He previously worked at Bonnier Publishing, with further experience in the publishing sector gained at Seren Books and the University of Wales Press. Robert holds an MA in English Literature from Cardiff University and BA in English Literature from Swansea University.

Significant research into how AI is transforming business has been and will continue to be conducted by consultancies, market research companies, academia and government services, plenty of which contributors have cited above. As a complement to this, what *AI Transforming Business* hopes to have uniquely achieved is an extended insight into the attitude and strategic approaches towards AI within large organizations, told from the perspectives of those at the very top. Decision-making authority is one thing that contributors to this book have in common, yet they are all working with the technology in different ways according to their role and industry. Authors prove that AI is bringing a paradigm shift to the business world – 'a phase change, and it's happening right now,' as Jon Catling concludes. We are entering a new era of business, one that is powered by AI. By identifying and bringing together key areas of common ground in the narrative, this chapter aims to provide a holistic look forward into the AI-enabled future of business.

Automation

Automation is a key concept discussed throughout this book. In the past two centuries, innovators focused on automating the physically repetitive, lower-skilled jobs of human workers; in the fourth industrial revolution, as Josh Sutton points out, 'the automation of knowledge work will transform traditional knowledge-based industries such as the law, medicine and finance.' There is, however, a pivotal difference in the nature of this automation, as it takes on a more complex and powerful meaning in the age of AI. Whereas previously technology was geared towards the automation and replacement of entire jobs – such as in the factories of the mid-60s – contributors illuminate how AI advancement focuses on the automation of specific tasks and therefore on the augmentation of humans within their jobs. As George Zarkadakis puts it, 'For some jobs artificial intelligence will be transformative, i.e. it will change the job in a radical way, eliminate the need for it, or possibly reinvent it. But for most jobs the effect of AI will be "augmentative", by enabling higher productivity and creativity.' Kalyan Kumar makes this point more emphatically: 'the power of AI is spectacular,' he says, 'But it pales in comparison to the power of "augmented intelligence" – a partnership between humans and machines.' It is case of man-plus-machine as opposed to man-versus-machine.

Customer service focus

It is no coincidence that the word 'customer' is mentioned more than one hundred times in this book. The potential for AI to transform customer service functions in major organizations is akin to its ability to improve internal efficiency and reduce costs. Jon Catling acknowledges that, for Las Vegas Sands, 'the key and most critical success factor is to be competent with our ability to speak to the customer.' But rather than negatively detract from the human touch, their AIConcierge embellishes the luxury customer experience and enables the organization to respond to the customer on-demand in a helpful way. In finance, too, AI is set to dramatically enhance customer service. Simeon Preston reveals how 'robo-advisors' in insurance will 'allow human advisors to deepen their customer relationships and give better-quality advice, and free up capacity so they can focus on the most valuable client interactions.' Kumar Srivastava foresees that 'client experience will be the differentiating and deciding factor in customer acquisition and retention.' Noel Lyons of Barclays builds his entire chapter on real-life experiments with AI in customer service.

Development of the technology

These senior technology leaders make clear that AI is pervading business, from the internal IT systems within companies through to the very outer touchpoints of hospitality. But intrinsic to the primary discussion of what AI can bring to a business is the development of solution providers themselves, and how they will advance the technology both to meet the demands of, and offer new solutions to, the enterprise. The ecosystem of solution providers and hierarchies of global enterprises enjoy a fully symbiotic relationship: while there is independent competition within each realm, the development of AI drives its implementation in enterprises and vice versa. NVIDIA's Kimberly Powell outlines the spectrum of today's innovators, with the giants of Google, Baidu, Facebook, Microsoft, Amazon and IBM at one end and nimble start-ups on the other. Over the next decade, though, she foresees start-ups becoming a dominant force in driving AI progress over the next decade due to three reasons: agility; innovation mindset, and attractiveness to top AI researchers and developers. In his chapter focusing on natural language, Michael Wei identifies three waves of development culminating in the era of 'Chatware'. 'The Google search bar will no longer be the default place for information,' he predicts. 'Upon looking for information, people can simply ask the machine.'

Looking ahead

These perspectives not only comprehensively assess the state of AI in business in 2017, they also illuminate what will happen in the future. Writing from NVIDIA's authoritative standpoint, Powell says that 'over the next three to five years, we predict that nearly every company in the world will be on their journey toward becoming an "AI enterprise"'. Srivastava is right to assert that 'The future is cut-throat and harsh', because for those market-leading businesses not willing to invest, innovate and implement, their lead will be squandered, however longstanding their superiority or reputation. Marc Lien advises with appropriate urgency:

'The world outside your organization is moving too quickly to allow for toe-dipping sequencing of initiatives.'

Beyond the realm of core industry verticals but at the core of every industry is cyber security, and as such it offers a useful stratospheric view of business. Darktrace CEO Nicole Eagan candidly readies enterprises for the fiercest technological battle the business world has ever seen. 'This is the future of AI in business: machines fighting machines in a battle for network dominance,' she tells us. By considering that business is companies fighting companies in a battle for market dominance, in this context we can infer that throwing AI into the gauntlet will make the battle fiercer as AI becomes more and more capable.

Eagan also discusses the idea of an 'unknown unknown' AI cyber-attack – a frightening prospect for network infrastructure. In human infrastructure, there are not only more tangible answers but also exciting opportunities. However, for businesses to identify new strategic paths in unknown AI-enabled terrain requires a unique combination of vision and practicality. While it is vital to assess the long-term potential of all forms of AI, we are, as Beena Ammanath makes clear, a long way away from developing a machine brain with human intelligence and capabilities.

In 2015-16, the most forward-thinking corporate CxOs were investigating the ecosystem and pinpointing the business processes that AI could improve, while carefully managing their expectations of the technology's current capabilities. This year, the rest of the enterprise world is playing catch-up while these business leaders are seeing ROI from their adoption of the technology. We are at the dawn of a new era for business – the beginning of a paradigm shift. In the coming three to five years, the paradigm shift will pass the halfway point, resulting in a global realization in the first world that AI is essential to the way that business is done. Once the paradigm shift is complete, every Fortune 1000 organization will have embraced AI and taken their place in the fourth industrial revolution. They will have a natural edge over organizations that continue to insist on a 'brick-and-mortar' approach to doing business.